THE ABINGDON WORSHIP ANNUAL 2010

CONTEMPORARY & TRADITIONAL
RESOURCES FOR WORSHIP LEADERS

The

ABINGDON
WORSHIP
ANNUAL
2010

EDITED BY MARY J. SCIFRES & B. J. BEU

Abingdon Press
Nashville

THE ABINGDON WORSHIP ANNUAL 2010
CONTEMPORARY AND TRADITIONAL RESOURCES FOR WORSHIP LEADERS

Copyright © 2009 by Abingdon Press

This book is printed on acid-free paper.

ISBN 978-0-687-65671-4

ISSN 1545-9322

All scripture quotations unless noted otherwise are taken from the New Revised Standard Version of the Bible, copyright 1989, Division of Christian Education of the National Council of the Churches of Christ in the United States of America. Used by permission. All rights reserved.

Prayers or litanies noted "THE MESSAGE" are adaptations of or based on THE MESSAGE. Copyright © Eugene H. Peterson, 1993, 1994, 1995, 1996, 2000, 2001, 2002. Used by permission of NavPress Publishing Group.

09 10 11 12 13 14 15 16 17 18—10 9 8 7 6 5 4 3 2 1

MANUFACTURED IN THE UNITED STATES OF AMERICA

CONTENTS

October

November

December

CD-ROM Contents

Calls to Worship
Contemporary Gathering Words and
Praise Sentences
Opening Prayers

CONTENTS

INTRODUCTION

Worship is a precious and intimate time in the life of every congregation. When your congregation entrusts you with the preparation and planning of worship, they grant you a great honor. We are grateful for the opportunity to share this honor as you invite us into your ministry of worship planning and preparation. In *The Abingdon Worship Annual 2010*, you will find words and ideas for focusing each week's worship service alongside prayers and litanies, and even an occasional drama idea for congregational participation. Included with this book are the full texts for each worship service on the enclosed CD ROM. This allows you to import printed prayers and responsive readings directly into your computer program for bulletin and program printing. Look for some surprises on the CD-ROM as well.

In *The Abingdon Worship Annual 2010*, you will find the words of many different authors, pastors, laypersons, and theologians. Some names you will recognize; others will be new to you. But each person has prayerfully studied the lections for each worship day, focused on a theme for that day, and composed words and a suggested flow for worship.

Since the contributing authors represent a wide variety of denominational and theological backgrounds, the words before you will vary in style and content. Feel free to combine or adjust the words within these pages to fit the needs of your congregation and the style of your worship services. (Notice the permission for reproduction of worship resource given on the copyright page of this book.)

This edition of the *Abingdon Worship Annual* contains words for worship for each Sunday of the lectionary year, along with suggestions for many of the "high" holy days. Each entry provides suggestions that follow an order of service that may be adapted to address your specific worship practice and format. Feel free to reorder or pick and choose the various resources to fit the needs of your worship services and congregations. Feel free, as well, to follow the suggested flow to ease your own task of planning and ordering worship.

Each entry follows a specific thematic focus arising from one or more of the week's scriptures. This focus, along with corresponding scripture imagery, is then carried out through each of the suggested prayers and litanies for a given worship service. For those who are working with contemporary worship services or who prefer informal words, alternative ideas for those settings are offered for each service as well. Each entry includes a Call to Worship and Opening Prayer; a Prayer of Confession and Assurance of Pardon or a Unison Prayer; a Response to the Word, Offertory, or Communion Resources; and a Benediction. Additional ideas are also provided throughout this resource. We have ordered each day's suggestion to fit a basic pattern of Christian worship, reflecting a flow that leads from a time of gathering and praise, into a time of receiving and responding to the word, and ending with a time of sending forth. The Praise Sentences and Contemporary Gathering Words fit the spontaneous and informal nature of many nontraditional worship styles and easily fit into the time for gathering and praise. They are often designed for use in worship without a printed program or bulletin.

In response to requests from many of our readers, we have provided a number of Communion liturgies as well. Some follow the pattern of the Great Thanksgiving; others are Prayers of Preparation and Consecration for the celebration of the Eucharist. You will find a full array of Communion liturgies on the CD-ROM. Consult the index for a listing of these many Communion resources and feel free to use them interchangeably throughout the corresponding seasons. For instance, the Communion service for February 21, 2010, could be used on any Sunday during Lent.

On the CD-ROM we are able to provide additional resources not found in this printed volume. For the next several years you will find the number of electronic resources included with the *Abingdon Worship Annual* enhanced and expanded. In this edition's CD-ROM you will find an annotated bibliography of suggested websites for worship planning, a short list of suggested songs or hymns for each worship day (hyperlinked to the entry for that day), and a wide variety of Communion prayers and liturgies. These suggestions are offered to ease your worship planning process and increase our creativity.

The Abingdon Worship Annual 2010 is only one piece of the puzzle you put together for worship preparation. For additional music suggestions you will want to consult *Prepare! A Weekly Worship Planbook for Pastors and Musicians* or *The United Methodist Music and Worship Planner*, each containing lengthy listings of lectionary-related hymns, praise songs, vocal solos, and choral anthems. As you plan lectionary-based worship, preachers will find *The Abingdon Preaching Annual 2010* an invaluable help. Worship planners and preachers can rely upon these resources to provide the words, the music, and the preaching guidance to plan integrated and coordinated worship services.

Many litanies, prayers, and calls to worship in *The Abingdon Worship Annual 2010* intersperse direct quotations from scripture with lines of text from other sources. In order to focus on the poetic nature of worship words, and to facilitate the ease of use, we do not indicate these direct quotations with quotation marks.

All contributions in *The Abingdon Worship Annual 2010* are based on readings from the *Revised Common Lectionary*. As you begin your worship planning, we encourage you to spend time with the scriptures for the day, reflecting upon them thoughtfully and prayerfully. Review the thematic ideas suggested in this resource and then read the many words for worship provided. Listen for the words that speak to you. Let this resource be the starting point for your worship planning. As the Spirit guides you and God's word flows through you, we pray that your worship planning may be meaningful and fulfilling for both you and your congregants. Trust God's guidance and enjoy a wonderful year of worship and praise with your congregations! We wish you God's blessings as you seek to share Christ's word and offer experiences of the Holy Spirit in your work and worship!

Mary J. Scifres and B. J. Beu, Editors

JANUARY 1, 2010

Watch Night / New Year
B. J. Beu

COLOR
White

SCRIPTURE READINGS
Ecclesiastes 3:1-13; Psalm 8; Revelation 21:1-6a;
Matthew 25:31-46

THEME IDEAS
Start with the end in mind. Where are we going and how
do we get there? Matthew reminds us that our actions
have eternal consequences. If we truly want to change our
lives we are charged to feed the hungry, clothe the naked,
visit the sick and imprisoned, and comfort those who
mourn. The new heaven and new earth may be in our
midst, but we need to treat one another lovingly if we
want to be part of it. In Ecclesiastes, God reminds us that
weeping, tearing down, and lying fallow will always be
part of the seasons and rhythms of life. As we look with
anticipation to the new year, we place our trust in the one
whose glory is beheld in the new heaven and new earth—
the one who will wipe away every tear.

INVITATION AND GATHERING

Call to Worship (Ecclesiastes 3, Psalm 8)
O Lord, our God,
   how majestic is your name!
As we journey through life,
   you are always with us.
In seasons of rejoicing,
   we do not laugh alone.
In seasons of mourning,
   we do not weep alone.
When the heavens open up,
   we behold your glory.
O Lord, our God,
   how majestic is your name!

Opening Prayer (Matthew 25)
Eternal God,
      as we enter into a new year,
      may our love for you be made known
         in our love for one another.
Help us forgive ourselves for past failings,
      even as we open our hearts
         to the possibilities that lie before us.
Guide our footsteps,
      that we may live as your beloved children,
         created but a little below the angels.

PROCLAMATION AND RESPONSE

Prayer of Confession (Matthew 25)
Holy God,
      we have forgotten how to love.
We praise you with our lips
      while remaining mute about your children—
         children who suffer from hunger
            and lack of shelter and warmth.
We lift up our eyes to delight in the starry heavens,
      while turning our gaze
         from the homeless and the needy.

Open our hearts to the welfare of others,
that we may live the promise
of a new heaven and a new earth. Amen.

Words of Assurance (Psalm 8)
Though we ask God with the psalmist:
"What is humanity that you are mindful of us?
Who are we that you care for us so deeply?"
You answer: "You are my children,
whom I have made but a little below the angels.
I have crowned you with glory and honor,
and will always love you."

Response to the Word (Ecclesiastes 3)
For everything there is a season. May this be a season of
new possibilities as we reflect on God's call to feed the
hungry, clothe the naked, visit the sick and imprisoned,
and comfort those who mourn.

THANKSGIVING AND COMMUNION

Offering Prayer (Matthew 25)
Mighty God,
as we bring you our offerings,
may we long to see,
not some beatific vision,
but the faces of those who hunger
and those who are sick or imprisoned;
may we yearn to behold the plight
of those society has left behind.
Only then may we see the face of Jesus.
May these offerings help heal our broken world.
May they heal our very selves. Amen.

SENDING FORTH

Benediction (Ecclesiastes 3, Matthew 25)
Every season in life is a blessing from God.
We rejoice in God's blessings!

3

Every purpose under heaven is part of God's plan.
We rejoice in God's purposes!
Every act of kindness to the least of God's children
is a kindness done to Christ.
**We rejoice in the chance to make a difference
in our world.**

CONTEMPORARY OPTIONS

Contemporary Gathering Words (Ecclesiastes 3)
God brings us to a new year.
Rejoice and be glad!
God brings us to new seasons of joy and hope.
Rejoice and be glad!
God shares our pain in seasons of sadness and loss.
Rejoice and be glad!
God brings us newness of life.
Rejoice and be glad!

Praise Sentences (Psalm 8)
God's name is above all names.
God's works are a wonder to behold.
God's love fills us with glory.
Praise God's holy name!

JANUARY 3, 2010

Epiphany of the Lord
Mary Petrina Boyd

COLOR
White

SCRIPTURE READINGS
Isaiah 60:1-6; Psalm 72:1-7, 10-14; Ephesians 3:1-12; Matthew 2:1-12

THEME IDEAS
The light of God's love shines brightly in these passages. Isaiah speaks of the radiance of God's glory drawing the nations together. The people come with rejoicing, bearing gifts of gold, and frankincense. Matthew tells of the magi, who followed the star to the Christ child, bearing gifts of gold, frankincense, and myrrh. Paul proclaims the boundless richness of Christ. This good news brings hope to those who despair. The psalmist reminds us that the true king will judge God's people with righteousness, bring justice to the poor, and save the lives of the needy. The infant in Bethlehem is this true king.

INVITATION AND GATHERING

Call to Worship (Isaiah 60, Matthew 2)
Arise, shine, for your light has come.
The glory of the Lord has risen upon you!
The glory of God shines in the darkness.

Lift up your eyes and look around.
Follow the star, wherever it leads!
Take the journey that leads to the child.
Let your hearts rejoice.
Be overwhelmed with joy!
We worship the Christ child,
the hope of the world.

Opening Prayer (Isaiah 60, Psalm 72, Ephesians 3, Matthew 2)

God of mystery,
    in the darkness of our world
        your light shines with grace and truth.
Open the eyes of our hearts
    to the glory of your love.
Speak your word of truth and joy.
May the mystery revealed in Jesus
    draw us closer to you.
May the wonder of your love
    fill us with wisdom and peace.
As we rejoice in your presence,
    teach us to seek justice and righteousness.
Fill our hearts to overflowing
    with your joy, your glory, your hope. Amen.

PROCLAMATION AND RESPONSE

Prayer of Confession (Psalm 72, Matthew 2)

God of starlight,
    shine your love
        into the darkness of our lives.
Preoccupied with ourselves,
    we forget the needs of others;
    we participate in systems that oppress;
    we accept violence as a way of life;
    we fail to respond to the cry of others.
May your love fall upon us
    like rain on the mown grass.

May your love wash away our indifference
and water the tender shoots
of our care and compassion.
Nourished in the sunlight of your love,
may we grow into people
who live in righteousness
and who work for justice
for all your children. Amen.

Words of Assurance (Ephesians 3)

In Jesus Christ, God has revealed the mystery that brings grace and forgiveness. The light of God's love transforms us so that we may act with boldness and confidence.

Passing the Peace of Christ (Psalm 72, Ephesians 3)

The mystery of Christ has been revealed to the world.
In that mystery, peace abounds.
Share the mystery of Christ's plentiful peace.

Response to the Word (Matthew 2)

We have seen your star, O God,
shining brightly over us
and all the peoples of the earth.
Teach us to trust your light.
Help us take risks,
that we might step out in faith
into the unknown.
Guide us to the place where you abide,
that we may be overwhelmed with joy
like the magi before us.
Guide us to the stable of your love,
that we may offer you
the gifts of our lives. Amen.

THANKSGIVING AND COMMUNION

Invitation to the Offering (Matthew 2)

The magi paid homage to the child, offering gifts of gold, frankincense, and myrrh. May we too bring the gifts of our lives and offer them in joy to Jesus Christ.

Offering Prayer (Psalm 72, Matthew 2)
> As long ago travelers laid their gifts
> > before the Christ child,
> > we too bring our gifts with great joy.
> Use our gifts for justice and righteousness,
> > that oppression and violence may cease
> > and peace may flourish.
> May the light of your love
> > shine through our living,
> > that suffering may end,
> > and all may rejoice
> > > in your gift of life. Amen.

Invitation to Communion (Matthew 2)
> By the light of the star,
> > God led travelers to the Christ child.
> When they saw the child
> > they were overwhelmed with joy.
> By the light of divine love,
> > God leads us to this holy meal.
> Gathered together,
> > we encounter the living Christ
> > and taste the deepest joy.

SENDING FORTH

Benediction (Matthew 2)
> Go forth and follow the star.
> When you have found the child,
> > tell the good news to the world.
> May the blessings of God's love
> > fill your hearts with overwhelming joy.

CONTEMPORARY OPTIONS

Contemporary Gathering Words (Isaiah 60, Matthew 2)
> The darkness is gone.
> > **Rejoice in the light!**

The star shines brightly.
Follow the star!
A child is born.
Bring your gifts!

Praise Sentences (Isaiah 60, Matthew 2)

Give glory to God!
Rejoice and be glad!
God's light shines!
Rejoice and be glad!
Jesus is born!
Rejoice and be glad!

JANUARY 10, 2010

Baptism of the Lord

Laura Jaquith Bartlett

COLOR

White

SCRIPTURE READINGS

Isaiah 43:1-7; Psalm 29; Acts 8:14-17; Luke 3:15-17, 21-22

THEME IDEAS

The psalmist depicts God's glory and majesty. Isaiah shows us God's strength—divine power is not just for show but is available to protect, support, and nurture God's beloved children. The story of Jesus' baptism evokes feelings of awe and wonder. It is impossible to picture the heavens opening and the Holy Spirit descending as a dove without total amazement! And yet, through our own sharing in the baptism of Christ, we are able to experience the intimacy of a God who loves us as precious children, a God who calls each of us by name.

INVITATION AND GATHERING

Call to Worship (Isaiah 43, Psalm 29)
Our God is a God of power and strength!
God has created each of us
with tender care.

Our God is a God of majesty and awe!
**God walks with each of us
every step of the way.**
Our God is a God of glory and wonder!
**God loves each of us
with tenderness and passion.**
Our God calls us each by name.
**God calls each of us
to unite in worship together!**

Opening Prayer (Psalm 29, Luke 3)
Holy God of glory and majesty,
    you have called us by name.
We pray in this moment
    for the courage and the strength
        to answer your call.
As we open our ears
    to hear the story of your Son's baptism,
    open our hearts also,
    that we may experience again
        the renewing power of rebirth
            in the Holy Spirit.
Inspire us in this time of worship,
    that we may claim our own identity
        as your beloved children.
We pray in the name of our brother, Jesus Christ. Amen.

PROCLAMATION AND RESPONSE

Prayer of Confession (Isaiah 43, Psalm 29, Luke 3)
Creator of the universe,
    we stand amazed at your power and glory.
We are eager to worship you and offer our praise,
    but we are often reluctant to answer
        when we hear you calling our name.
We sing our songs of tribute in the sanctuary,
    but shy away from the river,
        lest we be baptized
            with the fire of the Holy Spirit.

Forgive us when we forget your promise
  to be with us always, O God.
Renew us with the power of your ever-present love,
  and strengthen us to proclaim your justice
    throughout the world. Amen.

Words of Assurance (Isaiah 43)
Hear the words of our creator,
spoken through the prophet Isaiah:
  "I have called you by name.
  You are mine. Do not fear,
    for I have redeemed you."

Passing the Peace of Christ
As you greet those around you, look at each person and
offer these words from Isaiah: "You are precious in
God's sight."

Response to the Word (Isaiah 43, Luke 3)
Creator God, Holy One,
  you have made us in your image,
  and we are precious in your sight.
Jesus Christ, Son of God,
  we stand at the river,
  ready to share in your baptism.
Holy Spirit, Dove of Peace,
  set us on fire with the power of your love.

THANKSGIVING AND COMMUNION

Offering Prayer (Psalm 29, Acts 8)
Gracious God,
  we come today with joy for your baptism;
  we come with praise for your glory;
  we come with gratitude for your love.
As we offer these gifts to you,
  send your Spirit upon us,
  that our hands and our hearts
    may do your work in the world.

As we offer our lives to you,
bless us with your strength,
that we may join with you
to work for the blessing of peace
throughout the world. Amen.

Invitation to Reaffirm Our Baptismal Covenant

We gather today to worship and praise the God of awe and majesty. We come to encounter the God who knows us each by name and who walks with us in intimate love. We come to reaffirm the blessing we have received through our baptism. In baptism, we remember God's saving actions throughout history, and we have the opportunity to answer yes as God whispers our names. As a community of God, we gather today at the waters of baptism to reaffirm our commitment to Christ and to experience anew the transforming power of the Holy Spirit.

SENDING FORTH

Benediction (Isaiah 43)

You are each precious in God's sight.
**We go from this place,
claiming our identity as children of God.**
God has called you by name.
**We go into the world
to answer God's call. Alleluia!**

CONTEMPORARY OPTIONS

Contemporary Gathering Words (Isaiah 43)

(Three leaders are visible to begin the service. An unseen voice [amplified] speaks the words in bold print. The words are NOT printed for the congregation to see.)

Leader 1: *(Sounding bored)* Well, the clock says it's about time to start, so let's all just...

Voice: *(Interrupting)* **You are precious in my sight, and I love you.**

13

Leader 2:   What?! Who is...? Who are you talking to?
Voice: **I'm talking to you. You are my child, and I love you.**
Leader 1:   Hey, what's going on here? We're trying to start worship!
Voice: *You* **are precious in my sight, and I love you.**
Leader 3:   God, is that you? Are you really here?
Voice: **I am here, and I have called you because I love each of you.**
Leader 1:   God is here!
Leader 2:   God loves us!
Leader 3:   Let's worship God!

Praise Sentences (Psalm 29)

Ascribe to the Lord glory and strength!
The voice of the Lord is powerful and full of majesty.
The voice of the Lord thunders over mighty waters.
Worship the Lord in holy splendor!

JANUARY 17, 2010

Second Sunday after the Epiphany

Mary J. Scifres

COLOR
Green

SCRIPTURE READINGS
Isaiah 62:1-5; Psalm 36:5-10; 1 Corinthians 12:1-11;
John 2:1-11

THEME IDEAS
Focusing today's message on either Corinthians or John
seems so obvious. And yet, God's delight and steadfast
love for us, even in our frailty and sinfulness, dances off
the page in today's Hebrew Scripture readings. Whether
preaching on these, or on the blessing of spiritual gifts in
1 Corinthians 12 or on Jesus' miracle at the wedding celebration in Galilee, today's scriptures invite us to revel in
God's joyous love for us.

INVITATION AND GATHERING

Call to Worship (Isaiah 62)
Come to the celebration!
  We rejoice in the God of love!
God rejoices in your presence this day.
  Our delight is in our God.
God's delight is in you, my friends!
  Let us celebrate this joyous news!

Opening Prayer (Psalm 36, 1 Corinthians 12)

Fountain of life,
> we praise you for your steadfast love
> > and abiding faithfulness.

Dance with us,
> as we come into your presence with joy.

Celebrate with us,
> as we recognize and remember
> > your many gifts.

Call to us,
> as we listen for your voice
> > and learn to develop and share
> > > these gifts.

River of love,
> wash over us with your wisdom this day.

PROCLAMATION AND RESPONSE

Prayer of Confession (Isaiah 62, Psalm 36)

God of salvation and grace,
> do not forsake us in our sinfulness.

Forgive us and draw us closer to you.
In our desolation and desperation,
> walk with us and lead us
> > on the paths of righteousness.

Reclaim us and rename us,
> that we may know your presence
> > and sense your delight.

Words of Assurance (Psalm 36)

Drink from the river of Christ's grace,
> for in God we drink from the fountain of life.

God's steadfast love never wavers.
Rejoice, my friends!
In Christ's love, we are forgiven!

Passing the Peace of Christ (1 Corinthians 12)

Many and varied are we in this body of Christ. In Christ
Jesus, we are reconciled to God and to one another. In the

Spirit of God, we are made one. Let us delight in this unity as we share signs of peace and love.

Response to the Word or Prayer of Thanksgiving (Isaiah 62, Psalm 36, 1 Corinthians 12)

Joyous God,
>thank you for taking such delight in us
>>and for entrusting us
>>>with your many, generous gifts.

Strengthen us and guide us
>to proclaim your greatness in all that we say
>>and in all that we do.

Shine through our lives,
>that we may glorify you
>>each and every day.

THANKSGIVING AND COMMUNION

Invitation to the Offering (Isaiah 62, Psalm 36)

As we feast on the abundance of God's love and truth, we are invited to share that abundance with a world in need. Let us offer our gifts to God—symbols and tools of Christ's gracious love for the world. In these offerings, may others come to know God's great delight and love for us all!

Offering Prayer (Isaiah 62, Psalm 36, 1 Corinthians 12)

Generous God,
>we take delight in the many gifts
>>you have given us.

We rejoice in this opportunity
>to share these gifts with you
>>and your church.

We thank you for your steadfast love.

Continue to shine through us,
>that we may be a crown of your beautiful love
>>in this world. Amen.

17

SENDING FORTH

Benediction (Isaiah 62, Psalm 36, John 2)
Shine forth with Christ's love,
and God's glory will be revealed!

CONTEMPORARY OPTIONS

Contemporary Gathering Words (Psalm 36)
God's steadfast love extends to the heavens.
God's love is present here.
God's faithfulness rises to the clouds.
God's love is present here.
God's righteousness is as strong as the mountains.
God's love is present here.
God's judgments are great, full of wisdom and truth.
God's love is present here.
Come to the fountain, the river of life.
God's love is present here!

Praise Sentences (Isaiah 62)
Rejoice and be glad.
You are God's very delight!
Rejoice and be glad!
You are God's very delight!

JANUARY 24, 2010

Third Sunday after the Epiphany
B. J. Beu

COLOR
Green

SCRIPTURE READINGS
Nehemiah 8:1-3, 5-6, 8-10; Psalm 19; 1 Corinthians 12:12-31a; Luke 4:14-21

THEME IDEAS
With the psalmist, the church proclaims: "The law of the LORD is perfect, reviving the soul; the decrees of the LORD are sure, making wise the simple" (v. 7). The problem is, do we understand these teachings? The prophet Nehemiah read the laws of Moses with interpretation so that the people would understand. The psalmist attests that day and night pour forth speech and knowledge, but no words can contain their truth. Paul looks for the Spirit to bind the church of Corinth together through the power of Christian baptism because teachings on Christian unity fall flat. Even the people in Jesus' hometown cannot see the truth in front of their very eyes as Jesus reads from the scroll of Isaiah. They know all the words but none of the meaning. The precepts of God are perfect, but without help understanding them we are left little better off than we were before.

INVITATION AND GATHERING

Call to Worship (Nehemiah 8, Psalm 19)
Come! Hear the word of the Lord.
The Law of God is perfect, reviving the soul.
We hear but do not understand.
Who will teach us, that our hearts may rejoice?
Listen to the heavens, for they are telling
the glory of God. Day pours forth speech
and night declares knowledge.
Who can hear these voices—
voices that speak without words or speech?
Listen with your heart and you will hear.
Pray in the Spirit and you will perceive.
Amen, amen!

Opening Prayer (Luke 4)
God of wisdom,
we have come to sit at Jesus' feet—
to hear as he brings good news to the poor;
to rejoice as he proclaims
release to the captives,
recovery of sight to the blind,
and freedom for the oppressed;
to marvel as he declares the year of your favor.
Help us hear beyond the surface meaning
of your decrees, precepts, and teachings
to the spiritual depths they contain.
Teach us the music of the heavens—
the whispering of the land
and the roar of the seas,
that we may truly understand
the fullness of life
you have in store for us.

Passing the Peace of Christ (1 Corinthians 12:27)
"Now you are the body of Christ and individually mem-
bers of it." None of us is more important or more valued
by God than another. Let us rejoice in our place in the

body of Christ by turning to one another and passing the peace of Christ.

PROCLAMATION AND RESPONSE

Prayer of Confession (Nehemiah, 1 Corinthians 12)
Merciful God,
> we would rather glory in our gifts,
>> than acknowledge the gifts of others.

We hear your call to Christian unity,
> but cannot get past the slights
>> of our neighbors.

We lack the will and fortitude
> of the ancient Israelites
>> in the days of Nehemiah
>>> to listen to your precepts.

We lack even the desire to listen,
> as the heavens pour forth your praise
>> and the day and the night declare truth
>>> for all to hear.

Open our hearts to one another and to your world,
> especially the outcast and the marginalized.

Amen.

Words of Assurance (Nehemiah 8:10)
When the Israelites wept for their faults
> as the law of Moses was read,
> Nehemiah responded:
>> "Go your way, eat the fat and drink sweet wine
>>> and send portions of them to those
>>>> for whom nothing is prepared,
>>>> for this day is holy to our LORD;
>>> and do not be grieved,
>>>> for the joy of the LORD is your strength."

Introduction to the Word (Psalm 19:14)
"Let the words of my mouth and the meditation of my heart be acceptable to you, O LORD, my rock and my redeemer."

Response to the Word (Psalm 19:7-10)

With the psalmist, we proclaim:
"The law of the LORD is perfect, reviving the soul; the decrees of the LORD are sure, making wise the simple; the precepts of the LORD are right, rejoicing the heart; the commandment of the LORD is clear, enlightening the eyes; the fear of the LORD is pure, enduring forever; the ordinances of the LORD are true and righteous altogether. More to be desired are they than gold, even much fine gold; sweeter also than honey, and drippings of the honeycomb."

THANKSGIVING AND COMMUNION

Offering Prayer (Luke 4)

O Lord, our God,
    may the gifts we bring before you
      be outward and visible signs
        of the inward and spiritual grace
          you have blessed us with today;
    may they reflect our commitment
      to continue Jesus' mission:
        to bring good news to the poor,
        release to the captives,
        sight to the blind,
        and freedom to the oppressed.

SENDING FORTH

Benediction (1 Corinthians 12)

In one Spirit, we have all been baptized.
    Spirit, make us one!
In one faith, we have all been nurtured.
    Christ, make us one!
In one great love, we have all been saved.
    God, make us one!
Go with the blessing of God,
that we might all be one.

CONTEMPORARY OPTIONS

Contemporary Gathering Words (Psalm 19)

Listen! The heavens have something to tell us.
Give God the glory!
Ssh! The sun and moon have lessons to teach.
Give God the glory!
Hear the world around you!
What does it say?
Give God the glory!
Give God the glory!
Give God the glory!

Praise Sentences (Nehemiah 8)

The joy of the Lord is our strength.
The precepts of God are right,
rejoicing the heart.
The teachings of God are clear,
enlightening the eye.
The joy of the Lord is our strength.
Rejoice in the Lord!

JANUARY 31, 2010

Fourth Sunday after the Epiphany

Joanne Carlson Brown

COLOR

Green

SCRIPTURE READINGS

Jeremiah 1:4-10; Psalm 71:1-6; 1 Corinthians 13:1-13;
Luke 4:21-30

THEME IDEAS

Being a prophet is hard work! Jeremiah shies away from
the task. The psalmist is beset by foes. And the folks in
Jesus' hometown want to stone him. Where is all the love
Paul sings about in 1 Corinthians? It is there in the never-
ending, steadfast love of God that surrounds us from our
mother's womb to the earth's tomb. It is a love that calls
us to do things we feel inadequate to do. It is a love that
strengthens us and gives us courage and perseverance in
times of trial. It is a love that enables us to speak words of
truth to a questioning and sometimes hostile world. Love,
indeed, is the greatest of these.

INVITATION AND GATHERING

Call to Worship (Jeremiah 1, Luke 4)
Come! Hear the call of God:
"Speak of me to my people."

But we are just ordinary folks.
Who will listen?
"I will give you the words.
I will always be with you as you speak
my words of truth and justice and love."
We gather here to worship you,
to praise you for your loving presence,
and to be strengthened for the calling
you have given us.

Opening Prayer (Jeremiah 1, Psalm 71, 1 Corinthians 13, Luke 4)

O God,
    in the midst of the cacophony of voices
        that crush our spirit and deny our calling,
           voices that say,
               "Who do you think you are?"
    we come to hear your voice of affirmation;
    we come to hear your voice
        calling us to be and do
           what you have called us to be and do.
Let this time of worship quiet our fears,
    soothe our bruised souls,
    and energize us for ministry
        in and with your beloved world.
Let faith abide.
Let hope abide.
Let love abide—
    here in this sanctuary,
    here in our community,
    here in our world,
    but most of all, here in us. Amen.

PROCLAMATION AND RESPONSE

Prayer of Confession (Jeremiah 1, Luke 4)

God, who shapes the course of history,
    it is so hard to be a prophet.

25

We're just ordinary folks.
What do you expect us to do?
Who will listen to us anyway?
Even if they do, they'll only get mad.
You'd do better to find someone else—
    someone older, someone younger,
    someone more articulate,
    someone with more courage,
    someone with more faith.
But still we hear our call and your promise.
Forgive our feet of clay—
    when we try and evade your call,
    when we make excuses,
    when we doubt your presence,
    when we reject your prophets,
    when we reject ourselves.
In the opportunities and challenges in our lives,
    help us see that you are there,
        and help us respond in faith, hope, and love.

Words of Assurance (Psalm 71)
God is our rock and our fortress.
In God we find our hope and our strength.
We are always surrounded by God's forgiving love,
    a love that has known us from birth
        and will never leave us.

Passing the Peace of Christ (1 Corinthians 13)
The love of God surrounds us.
    We rejoice in that love.
Let us greet one another in that love, in that hope,
in that abiding faith.

Response to the Word (Jeremiah 1, 1 Corinthians 13)
Hear God's word—
    the words of call,
    the words of promise,
    the words of faith,
    the words of hope,

the words of love.
Live God's word—
the words of life.

THANKSGIVING AND COMMUNION

Invitation to Offering (Jeremiah 1, Luke 4)
We have been called to speak and to live out the radical,
abiding love of God in the world. We do so by offering all
that we are, all that we do, and all that we have, knowing
that God will use us and our gifts to bring the beloved
community ever closer to being realized in this world.

Offering Prayer (Jeremiah 1, 1 Corinthians 13)
Gracious and loving God,
  receive our gifts of self and substance.
They have belonged to you
  since our very beginning.
We give them freely, joyfully, prayerfully.
With them we praise you.
With them we celebrate the great power
  that is love—
    a love that abides always,
    a love that radically transforms,
    a love that makes us whole.

SENDING FORTH

Benediction (Jeremiah 1, Psalm 71, 1 Corinthians 13,
Luke 4)
Go forth, celebrating faith.
Go forth, celebrating hope.
Go forth, celebrating love.
Go forth to be the transformed people
  that God calls us to be.
Go forth to transform the world—
  in times of prosperity,
  but most especially, in times of disbelief,
    hostility, fear, and rejection.

Go forth with the knowledge
that you are always surrounded
by the presence of our steadfast, loving God,
our rock and our redeemer.

CONTEMPORARY OPTIONS

Contemporary Gathering Words (Jeremiah 1, 1 Corinthians 13, Luke 4)

People of God, come hear the good news.
But we hear the voice of God calling us
to places we are afraid to go.
People of God, take courage in the loving,
sustaining presence of God.
We are here to find strength and courage,
to find faith and hope, to lean on
the everlasting, loving arms of God.

Praise Sentences (Jeremiah 1, Psalm 71, 1 Corinthians 13)

O God, you are our rock and our fortress.
In you we find strength to go on.
We praise you for the gifts of faith, hope, and love.
We will live out our call to be all
you have created us to be.

FEBRUARY 7, 2010

Fifth Sunday after the Epiphany

Shari Jackson Monson

COLOR

Green

SCRIPTURE READINGS

Isaiah 6:1-8 (9-13); Psalm 138; 1 Corinthians 15:1-11;
Luke 5:1-11

THEME IDEAS

Today's scriptures remind us that being confronted with
God's holiness and majesty can be terrifying. Isaiah has a
vision of the Lord surrounded by seraphim and cries out
that he is lost. Peter, likewise, perceives Jesus' holiness and
can hardly bear to be in the presence of God's anointed.
Paul grieves and shakes at the thought of his own prior
persecution of the church. And the psalmist knows full
well the glory of God and the wrath that God can visit on
the unrighteous. God calls us to service, but that call can
seem terrifying. Is it any wonder that God is always saying, "Be not afraid"?

INVITATION AND GATHERING

Call to Worship (Psalm 138)
Praise the Lord with all your heart.
May all the peoples praise you, O God.

Worship the Lord alone, for there is no god
like our God.
**We worship you, O God, for your faithful love
is like no other.**
Call on the Lord, and God will answer.
Be with us, O God, in our time of need.
Praise the Lord with all your heart.
May all the peoples praise you, O God.

Opening Prayer (Isaiah 6, Luke 5)
Gracious Lord,
    we come into your house
        in awe and amazement.
May you find us worthy of your call.
Confronted with your holiness,
    we feel beneath your attention.
Yet, like the crowds on the lakeshore in Galilee,
    our spirits long to hear from you,
        to learn your ways,
        to be made bold by your truth.
Help us best our fears,
    that we may not shrink from your presence,
        but may be emboldened
            through our worship this day. Amen.

PROCLAMATION AND RESPONSE

Prayer of Confession (Isaiah 6, Luke 5)
Lord of all, exalted and lifted up,
    you reside on a throne of glory
        with seraphim crying, "Holy, holy, holy."
How can we stand in your presence?
We are people made unclean
    by our callused and rebellious hearts.
We revel in games of one-upmanship,
    and delight when others fall in disgrace.
Our thoughts are not your thoughts.

Our actions fall short
  of the glory to which we are called.
Bring us to your mercy seat
  in this, our hour of need.
Hear us as we confess the disquiet of our hearts.
(Pause for a moment of silence.)
Blot out our guilt, O God,
  and grant us the courage
    to embrace the ways of life. Amen.

Words of Assurance (1 Corinthians 15)
By the grace of God,
  we receive forgiveness and are made new
    in our risen Lord.
Hold firm this day to what you have received
  through the mercies of God.

Passing the Peace of Christ
Hold firm to the grace of Christ.
Hold firm and live!

Response to the Word (Isaiah 6)
Like Isaiah before us, God has blotted out our sin. In response to God's call, let us proclaim with the prophet's zeal: "Here am I; send me!"
(B. J. Beu)

THANKSGIVING AND COMMUNION

Invitation to the Offering
O Lord,
  you ask us to examine our lives:
    what we find precious,
    what we value,
    what we hold on to;
  you ask us to receive your saving love:
    your many blessings,
    your surprising and startling gifts,
    your offer of life renewed.

With gratitude and thanks,
>   we return to you
>   a portion of the bounty
>   with which you bless us.
> As we take up our offering,
>   receive our gifts to your glory. Amen.

Offering Prayer or Communion Prayer
> Holy God,
>   take these, the gifts of our hands,
>   bless and multiply them
>   for the sake of your kingdom. Amen.

SENDING FORTH

Benediction (1 Corinthians 15)
> Live as God's people,
>   through the power of the Holy Spirit.
> Hold firm to the word preached to you,
>   through the grace of the risen Lord.
> Lift up your hands and hearts
>   and receive God's blessing.
> In the name of the Father, and the Son,
>   and the Holy Spirit,
>   go forth to share the truth of the gospel
>   to a watching world.

CONTEMPORARY OPTIONS

Contemporary Gathering Words (Psalm 138)
> Praise leaps from our grateful hearts.
>   **Lord, you are worthy of our praise.**
> Worship flows from our sense of awe of your glory.
>   **Lord, you are holy and exalted.**
> Thankfulness grows from hearing your call.
>   **Lord, we gather to praise you.**
>   **We come to worship you, Lord of all!**

Praise Sentences (Isaiah 6, 1 Corinthians 15)
Holy, holy, holy is the Lord of hosts.
Our God is greatly to be praised.
Holy, holy, holy is Christ our King.
Our God is greatly to be praised.
Holy, holy, holy is the Spirit of the living God.
Our God is greatly to be praised.
(B. J. Beu)

FEBRUARY 14, 2010

Transfiguration Sunday
Shelley Cunningham

COLOR
White

SCRIPTURE READINGS
Exodus 34:29-35; Psalm 99; 2 Corinthians 3:12–4:2; Luke 9:28-36

THEME IDEAS
"Mountaintop experiences"—it's the phrase we use to describe those ultimate highs in life. In these passages, Moses encounters God on Mount Sinai and the disciples view Jesus' transfiguration on a mountaintop. Both experiences offer glimpses of the awesome power and mystery of God's presence. Yet the reality of mountaintop experiences is that we don't live there—at some point, we have to come down. How do we sustain a mountaintop experience of God in everyday life? How do we find God's presence each and every day? The psalmist suggests continual worship and praise, whereas Paul encourages us to live and serve with faithfulness and integrity, for our ability to do so comes from God.

INVITATION AND GATHERING
Call to Worship (Psalm 99)
The Lord reigns.
Let the nations tremble.

The Lord reigns.
Let them praise God's holy name.
The Lord reigns.
Let the peoples rejoice in awe and wonder.
The Lord reigns.
Let them shout in exaltation!

Opening Prayer (2 Corinthians 3, Luke 9)
Radiant Lord,
   you shine with purity, power, and truth.
Your mercy reflects your compassion,
   your care, and your love.
Transform us into your image
   as we seek to follow you.
Use us to make your presence known
   throughout the world.
In your strong name we pray. Amen.

PROCLAMATION AND RESPONSE

Prayer of Confession (Luke 9)
Lord,
   you call us to draw near,
   yet we fail to hear your voice.
We sleepwalk through life,
   ignoring the needs of people all around us
     and worrying about our own desires.
Forgive us:
   when we shut out the call
     to climb into your presence;
   when we make excuses
     to put off that journey.
Have mercy on us, O Lord,
   as we silently open our hearts
     and confess our sins:
(Time of silence)
Hear our pleas, O God,
   and lift us to newness of life. Amen.

Words of Assurance (2 Corinthians 3, Psalm 99, Luke 9)
We worship a forgiving God,
   whose mercy is never ending,
   whose heart abounds in steadfast love.
Because of the love of Jesus Christ,
   nothing can separate us
     from the love of God.

Passing the Peace of Christ (Luke 9)
In the face of a stranger, in the greeting of a friend, we see
our Lord, Jesus Christ. In the love of Christ, welcome
those around you today.

Response to the Word (Luke 9)
Lord, it is good to be here—
   to hear your word,
   to share your story.
Help us see your Son for who he really is.
Help us listen to him,
   receive his forgiveness,
     and walk in his light.

THANKSGIVING AND COMMUNION

Invitation to the Offering (Exodus 34, 2 Corinthians 3)
In days of old, God was seen as far from the people.
But we know Christ, and in him we know God.
When we share what we have out of love,
   our hearts grow closer to God,
     and we shine with Christ's glory.
Let us offer our gifts to God today.

Offering Prayer (2 Corinthians 4)
Generous God,
   it is through your mercy
     that we have this ministry—
       the ministry of our talents and treasure,
       the ministry of our passion and purpose.

Strengthen our hearts for your service,
and accept the grateful offerings
we lay before you. Amen.

SENDING FORTH

Benediction (Luke 9)
Led by the Spirit,
go forth in God's love.
Illumined by the Spirit,
shine with Christ's light. Amen.

CONTEMPORARY OPTIONS

Contemporary Gathering Words (Luke 9, 2 Corinthians 3)
Will you come to the highest mountain?
We come to worship the Lord.
Jesus is waiting, waiting to greet you.
Jesus, we come. Jesus, we're here.
Come!
We come to worship the Lord.

Praise Sentences (Luke 9, 2 Corinthians 3)
You are so good, Lord!
Your love warms our hearts.
You are so good, Lord!
Your love shows us the way.
You are so good, Lord!
Your love shines like the sun.
You are so good, Lord!
You are so good!

FEBRUARY 17, 2010

Ash Wednesday
Jamie Greening

COLOR
Purple or Gray

SCRIPTURE READINGS
Joel 2:1-2, 12-17; Psalm 51:1-17; 2 Corinthians 5:20b–6:10, Matthew 6:1-6, 16-21

THEME IDEAS
Ash Wednesday is a somber reminder that life is fleeting and sin is always with us. The theme of repentance finds expression as we contemplate our mortality with the powerful symbols of ashes and sackcloth. The lections remind us of our corporate guilt, while helping the individual worshiper focus upon her or his own guilt before the Almighty Forgiver. In the Gospel reading, Christ reminds us that fasting and repentance are a part of the Christian experience. Therefore, we too are expected to engage in the difficult spiritual discipline of self-denial. We too are invited to return to God.

INVITATION AND GATHERING

Call to Worship (Joel 2)

(A single trumpet may sound a somber note before or after each refrain, "Blow the trumpet!")

Blow the trumpet!
Sanctify a fast.
Blow the trumpet!
Gather the people in solemn assembly.
Blow the trumpet!
Call the people to repentance.
Blow the trumpet!
Weep with godly sorrow.
Blow the trumpet!
Return to God with all your heart.

Opening Prayer (Psalm 51, 2 Corinthians 5–6, Matthew 6)

O Lord,
   open our hearts,
     that we may acknowledge our failings;
   open our lips,
     that we may declare your praise.
Though we all fall short,
   we praise you in the name of Christ,
     who takes away our sin
     and makes us walk
       in the paths of righteousness
May our Lenten fast
   begin not with dismal faces
   or with sorrowful frowns,
   but with faces aglow
     in the oil of your Holy Spirit. Amen.

PROCLAMATION AND RESPONSE

Prayer of Confession (Psalm 51)

Merciful God,
   cleanse us with hyssop;

wash us white as snow.
You desire truth in our inner being—
truth about our many failings:
    lust *(pause)*,
    greed *(pause)*,
    oppression *(pause)*,
    violence *(pause)*,
    intolerance *(pause)*,
    racism *(pause)*.
Purge our sins
    with the atoning hyssop
    of Christ the Lord. Amen.

Words of Assurance (Joel 2)

The promise of God is clear.
When we return to the Lord,
    God is gracious and merciful,
    slow to anger and abounding in steadfast love.
When we return to the Lord with weeping and fasting,
    God forgives our sin and blesses us
        with a renewed and deepened relationship
        with the Almighty.

Passing the Peace of Christ (2 Corinthians 5–6)

Say to yourself, "Now is the time of my salvation." Say to
your friend, "Now is the time of your salvation." Say to all
those around you, "Now is the time of our salvation."

Response to the Word (Psalm 51)

By confessing our sin
    our joy has been restored.
By praying to our forgiving God
    our joy has been restored.
Our joy has been restored,
    for we have been forgiven.
Our joy has been restored,
    for we have heard the word of God.

THANKSGIVING AND COMMUNION

Offering Prayer (Psalm 51)
What would make you happy, God?
We know it is not sacrifice.
Our cash is cold and hard and heartless
    as it drops into the offering plate.
You have told us what is pleasing,
    a broken and contrite heart.
Receive this day our sacrifice of praise,
    as we give to you
        the very depths of our souls.
In Jesus' name, we pray. Amen.

Invitation to Ashes (Optional)
(All kneeling. Before the liturgy begins, consider reading from John Donne's "No Man is an Island.")
Remember, from dust you came,
and to dust you shall return.
    We remember.
(Silence)
Remember, you are mortal, and this life will end.
    We remember.
(Silence)
Remember, you are incomplete without Christ.
    We remember.
(Silence)
Remember, God turns ashes into beauty
and sorrow into joy.
    We remember.

SENDING FORTH

Benediction (Matthew 6 and 2 Corinthians 5–6)
In the depth of our hearts,
    we have drawn strength from God.
From that strength,
    we overcome the challenges of life.

CONTEMPORARY OPTIONS

Contemporary Gathering Words (Joel 2)

Return to the Lord:
> leave the comforts,
> give up the latte,
> forsake the silk,
> turn off the technology.

Return to the Lord:
> put on the sackcloth,
> feel the ash,
> walk in contemplation,
> journey to the depths.

Return to the Lord:
> rend your hearts,
> forsake evil,
> avoid pretense,
> refuse to go numb.

Return to the Lord:
> put on the Father,
> feel the Spirit,
> walk forty days with Jesus,
> take time to be holy.

Praise Sentences

Our mouths declare your praise, O God.
In you we find forgiveness.
Our mouths declare your praise, O God.
In you we find spiritual awareness.
Our mouths declare your praise, O God.
In you we find true worship.

FEBRUARY 21, 2010

First Sunday in Lent
Mary J. Scifres

COLOR

Purple

SCRIPTURE READINGS

Deuteronomy 26:1-11; Psalm 91:1-2, 9-16;
Romans 10:8b-13; Luke 4:1-13

THEME IDEAS

As the Lenten journey begins, today's scriptures connect us to the journeys of generations past: Abraham and Moses, Sarah and Miriam, David and Solomon, Paul and all those who followed God on this journey of faith. All these, though faithful, failed in many ways and fell into temptation. It is here that we lift up the journey of Jesus. We are challenged to find the strength and courage to resist those temptations that would lead us astray or trap us in the wilderness of our confusion. We are invited to call upon the One who saves all of us, who shelters and guards us, and who strengthens us for this journey.

INVITATION AND GATHERING

Call to Worship (Psalm 91)
Come! Dwell in the shelter of God,
the shelter of holy love.
Trust in Christ Jesus,
our Refuge and our Strength.
Abide in God's house, the household of love.

Opening Prayer (Luke 4, Lent)
God, our Guide and Guardian,
lead us on this journey of faith.
Through the days and weeks of Lent,
help us walk your path
to the cross;
strengthen us to resist the demons
that would lead us astray.
Walk with us, Christ Jesus.
Be our shelter and our salvation,
even as we seek to be your disciples.

PROCLAMATION AND RESPONSE

Call to Confession (Romans 10)
Believe with your heart...
and the path to God will be clear.
Confess with your lips...
and salvation will be given to you.

Prayer of Confession (Luke 4)
Gracious God,
you know the difficult paths we tread;
you know the challenges we face.
Forgive us,
when we wander away
from your guidance.
Reclaim us,
when we seek other gods
that lead to our own destruction.

Guide us back to you,
that we may rest in your shelter.
Strengthen our resolve,
that we may face the demons of our lives
and courageously resist the temptations
that blind us to your love.
In hope and trust, we pray. Amen.

Words of Assurance (Romans 10)

Because we trust in the midst of our doubt,
God's path is laid before us.
Because we hope in the face of our sin,
salvation is ours!
In the name of Christ,
we are all forgiven and reclaimed by God!

Response to the Word or Benediction (Psalm 91)

Blessed are you who abide in the shelter of God!
Christ, our refuge and fortress,
guards our way.
Christ, who commands the angels, walks with us.
The Most High dwells within and among us.
Go forward in faith, confidence, and trust.
We journey through Lent with Easter hope.

THANKSGIVING AND COMMUNION

Invitation to the Offering (Deuteronomy 26)

We, who know the promises of God, are invited to share
the good news with others. Come; let us offer the first
fruits of the harvest, the best of all our gifts, as a bounty of
love to God.

Offering Prayer (Luke 4)

Gracious God,
we bring this offering
for a world that needs more than bread.
Transform our dollars and coins into your gifts:
bread for the journey,

food for the hungry,
hope for the despairing,
and opportunity for the discouraged.
Transform our lives,
that we may walk with Christ
and offer your love to the world. Amen.

Great Thanksgiving (Deuteronomy 26, Lent)

Lift up your hearts!
We lift them up to God!
Celebrate God's love!
It is right to give God our thanks and praise!
We give thanks and praise to you,
our Guide and Guardian!
We celebrate your creative presence,
which has called forth this glorious earth
and the heavens above.
We praise and glorify you
for creating us in your very image.
We celebrate the long history
when you traveled with us,
guiding us along the way.
From the days of wandering Arameans
and brave young prophets,
you have shown us the path
of justice and righteousness.
In the fullness of time, your presence
dwelt with us in Jesus the Christ,
showing us the way of strength and trust.
Even when faced with death, Christ gave thanks
and blessed the fruit of this, your good earth,
offering not only bread and wine,
but the bread of life and the wine of salvation.
We remember his invitation to abundant life:
"Take, eat; this is my body, broken for you.
Take, drink; this is my life poured out for you
and for many."

As we walk this journey of life,
  we remember these gifts
  as we proclaim the mystery of faith.
  Christ has died.
  Christ is risen.
  Christ will come again.

Prayer of Consecration
  God of love,
    send your Holy Spirit upon us.
  Touch these gifts with your Spirit,
    that they may be signs of love and life
      to a world full of hatred and death. Amen.

SENDING FORTH

Benediction (Luke 4)
  As we leave this place, we continue the journey.
  Christ leads us upon the way.

CONTEMPORARY OPTIONS

Contemporary Gathering Words (Deuteronomy 26, Luke 4)
  Come, all you wanderers and seekers.
  Our ancestors wandered and sought.
  Our Savior wandered and sought.
  Come, all you wanderers and seekers.
  Christ guides us to the love of God.

Praise Sentences (Romans 10)
  Everyone who calls on the name of Christ
  is promised salvation and love!
    Everyone who calls on the name of Christ
    is promised salvation and love!
  Call on the Lord in faithful trust.
    We call on the Lord this day!

FEBRUARY 28, 2010

Second Sunday in Lent
Laura Jaquith Bartlett

COLOR
Purple

SCRIPTURE READINGS
Genesis 15:1-12, 17-18; Psalm 27; Philippians 3:17–4:1; Luke 13:31-35

THEME IDEAS
Today's Scripture readings remind us of the enduring faithfulness of God. If only our faith were strong enough to trust God every moment! Through the Scriptures, we discover that God stays with us even in our doubt. Be inspired by these striking images of comfort: the Lord protects me (Psalm 27); Jesus seeks to gather us under his wings (Luke 13). Through the coming of Jesus Christ, we know firsthand the power of God's kept promises!

INVITATION AND GATHERING

Call to Worship (Genesis 15, Psalm 27, Luke 13)
Wait for the Lord; be strong!
The promises of God will never be broken.
With God as our light, what is there to fear?
The promises of God will never be broken.

Blessed is the one who comes in the name
of the Lord!
The promises of God will never be broken.

Opening Prayer (Genesis 15, Psalm 27, Philippians 3)

God of promises fulfilled,
    we gather as descendants of Abraham;
    we stand before you
        as faithful testimony to your covenant;
    we assemble as living proof
        that your love for humanity
            knows no limits.
When we feel overwhelmed
    by the stresses of daily life,
    we need only look at the stars in the sky
        to remember your abiding faithfulness.
When we are overcome with despair
    by the pain of war and poverty in our world,
    we need only see the light of a single candle
        to remember the one you sent
            as our light, our strength, and our salvation.
We pray now in the name of that light,
    Jesus Christ. Amen.

PROCLAMATION AND RESPONSE

Prayer of Confession (Genesis 15, Psalm 27)

Eternal God,
    we are quick to join
        Abram's doubt and impatience,
    but we find it difficult to copy
        Abraham's faith and trust.
We want to believe your promises,
    but the here-and-now problems of daily life
        consume our focus
        and erode our faith.
Open our eyes to your light.
Open our hearts to your love.

Open our minds to your possibilities.
Speak to us today, O God,
   and strengthen our faith,
      that we, too, may know
         the everlasting power of your love.

Words of Assurance (Psalm 27)
When God is with us, whom shall we fear?
The God of salvation will never forsake you.
God's patience knows no limits.
Wait for the Lord.
Be strong and take heart.

Response to the Word (Psalm 27, Luke 13)
(Use this as a responsive reading in the bulletin, or have eight readers in the midst of the congregation each speak one of the bolded attributes of the proper noun that the worship leader speaks. Allow plenty of time between each word.)

Light:
   shining, burning, beacon, warmth, glowing, showing, salvation, love.
Rock:
   stronghold, fortress, foundation, strength, protection, redeemer, salvation, love.
Hen:
   mother, parent, safety, care, protection, nurture, salvation, love.
Jesus:
   prophet, blessing, transformer, promise, fulfillment, savior, salvation, love.

THANKSGIVING AND COMMUNION

Offering Prayer (Genesis 15, Luke 13)
Faithful God,
   you have kept your promises to us.
Our lives give witness
   to your abundant blessings.

May we faithfully keep
 our promises to you.
Strengthen our commitment
 to live as true disciples of Jesus Christ.
Your love sustains us,
 guides us, and empowers us.
Take these gifts as signs of our promise
 to give ourselves completely into your care—
  to live without fear;
  to trust your love without reservation. Amen.

Prayer after Communion (Genesis 15, Philippians 3)
Dear God,
 we give thanks for your promised care.
In the sharing of this meal,
 we participate in the fulfillment
 of your greatest promise.
We celebrate our kinship
 with your Son, Jesus Christ,
 made known to us
  in the breaking of the bread of life
  and the sharing of the cup of salvation.
May your Holy Spirit strengthen us,
 that we may go into the world
  to imitate Christ and live as witnesses
  of your promised love. Amen.

SENDING FORTH

Benediction
Go in the love of God,
whose promises are never broken.
We go in the light of Christ,
whose love transforms us.
Go in the power of the Holy Spirit,
whose fire sustains and encourages us.
We go now into the world as witnesses
of God's love, light, and power.

CONTEMPORARY OPTIONS

Contemporary Gathering Words (Psalm 27)

Light, space, zest—that's God!
With God on our side, we're fearless,
afraid of no one and nothing.
Come on in—we're in God's place!
We're ready to offer anthems and songs
that will raise the roof!
Let's join in making music to God.
We want to sing God-songs!

Praise Sentences (Philippians 3)

Brothers and sisters, Christ is our example.
Christ is our life.
Brothers and sisters, Christ is our salvation.
Christ is our savior.
Brothers and sisters, Christ is the Lord.
Christ is the Lord!

MARCH 7, 2010

Third Sunday in Lent

B. J. Beu

COLOR

Purple

SCRIPTURE READINGS

Isaiah 55:1-9; Psalm 63:1-8; 1 Corinthians 10:1-13;
Luke 13:1-9

THEME IDEAS

God desires nothing more than that we come to the waters
and drink. God offers us, without price, the bread of life
and the sweet wine of salvation, but we often seek that
food and drink that does not satisfy. Though the everlasting covenant God made with David holds still, we do
not get a free pass—the unrighteous are called to change
their ways, and woe to us if we too quickly count ourselves among the righteous! This third Sunday in Lent
makes it clear that we must repent or perish. Jesus' parable of the fig tree echoes Isaiah's challenge, "Let the
wicked forsake their way" (v. 7). Paul warns that our ancestors ate spiritual food but strayed from God's paths
and perished. We are called to repentance that we may
partake of the abundant life God offers us.

INVITATION AND GATHERING

Call to Worship *(Isaiah 55, Psalm 63)*

The table is set. The banquet is laid.
Our souls hunger and thirst for God!
The Host is ready to welcome us here.
Our souls hunger and thirst for God!
"Return to me, return to me," says the Lord.
Our souls hunger and thirst for God!

Opening Prayer *(Psalm 63, 1 Corinthians 10)*

Lord of overflowing abundance,
    you are our God.
Our souls thirst for you
    like travelers in a dry and weary land.
We praise you with joyful lips
    and bless you with uplifted hands.
Guard us when we stand for what is right,
    lest we fall to our disgrace.
Test our courage in the face of evil,
    but save us from the time of trial,
        that we may be worthy disciples of your Son,
        our rock and our foundation. Amen.

PROCLAMATION AND RESPONSE

Prayer of Confession *(Isaiah 55, Psalm 63)*

Merciful God,
    we are so thirsty!
Yet when offered refreshment
    from the waters of life,
        we rely on our own means
        and end up drinking sand.
Heal our hardness of heart
    and help us seek you
        while you may be found,
        that we may abide in your steadfast love,
        now and forevermore. Amen.

Words of Assurance (1 Corinthians 10, Luke 13)

God is our help in times of trial.
If we put our trust in Christ,
    God will help us stand.
Even if we have not borne good fruit in the past,
    Christ works to help us bear good fruit
        in the time before us.

Response to the Word (Isaiah 55)

Seek the Lord while God may be found. Call upon the
Lord while God is near. Let the wicked forsake their ways.
Let the unrighteous shun the ways that destroy community. Let us return to the Lord, who is merciful and par-
dons the transgressions of those who amend their lives.

THANKSGIVING AND COMMUNION

Offering Prayer (Luke 13)

Loving God,
    you have set the table
        and have given us every good thing.
In gratitude for your kindness and mercy,
    receive our thanks and offerings.
Accept our hearts into your keeping,
    that our lives may bear good fruit
        as we may enter into your glory. Amen.

SENDING FORTH

Benediction or Call to Worship (Isaiah 55, Psalm 63)

Seek the Lord while God may be found.
    Call upon the Lord while God is near!
Forsake the ways that lead to death.
    Embrace the paths that lead to life.
Return to the Lord, who abounds in mercy.
    It is never too late to return to God!
Seek the Lord while God may be found.
    Call upon the Lord while God is near!

CONTEMPORARY OPTIONS

Contemporary Gathering Words (Isaiah 55)

Turn to God now, for the Lord is here.
Give us a minute!
You may not have a minute.
Who knows when it will be too late?
Too late?!
Do you really want to miss it—
the food and drink that nourishes
body and soul?
Sounds expensive!
How much will it cost?
God's love comes without price—
but it's not free. We have to turn to God
with our whole heart.
God's mercy will save us! Amen.

Praise Sentences (Psalm 63, 1 Corinthians 10)

Praise God with joyful lips.
Glory to Christ who waits with us
in the bitter watches of the night.
Praise God with a contrite heart.
Glory to Christ who waits with us
in the bitter watches of the night.
Praise God with a searching spirit.
Glory to Christ who waits with us
in the bitter watches of the night.

MARCH 14, 2010

Fourth Sunday in Lent
Mary J. Scifres

COLOR
Purple

SCRIPTURE READINGS
Joshua 5:9-12; Psalm 32; 2 Corinthians 5:16-21;
Luke 15:1-3, 11b-32

THEME IDEAS
New opportunities, new creation, new life. The newness
Christ offers is a gift that comes from forgiveness and reconciliation—a gift that brings joy and hope. When we embrace and integrate these gifts into our lives, we are
moved to celebrate and rejoice. When we embrace and integrate these gifts into our ministries, we are strengthened
to become ambassadors for Christ. When we embrace and
integrate these gifts into our beliefs, we are able to become
friends, fathers, mothers, sisters, and brothers who forgive
and offer new beginnings to others.

INVITATION AND GATHERING

Call to Worship (1 Corinthians 5, Luke 15)
The old has passed away.
Our yesterdays are past and gone.
Today is alive with fresh possibilities.

The present is vibrant with new opportunities.
In Christ, we are offered newness of life.
In Christ, we are offered renewal of hope.
In Christ, we are given forgiveness and grace.
In Christ, we live in celebration and joy.

Opening Prayer (Joshua 5, 2 Corinthians 5, Luke 15)

God of forgiveness and grace,
  thank you for your warm and loving welcome.
Open our hearts,
  that we may receive your grace and peace.
Bless us and renew us,
  that we may live as the new creations.
Inspire us to be your kingdom on this earth,
  that we may be your promised land—
    with actions that nourish like milk;
    with words that soothe like honey. Amen.

PROCLAMATION AND RESPONSE

Prayer of Confession (Luke 15)

God of grace and love,
  forgive us when we wander away
    from your promises;
  forgive us when we withhold from others
    the forgiveness we seek for ourselves.
Welcome us into your loving embrace.
Warm us with your grace,
  that we may reach out with loving arms
    to a world in need of your compassion,
    a world in need of your love.
In Christ's name, we pray. Amen.

Words of Assurance (1 Corinthians 5, Luke 15)

Rejoice! She who was lost has been found.
Sing aloud! He who was dead is alive.
In Christ, you are a new creation.
In Christ, you are a new creation.

Passing the Peace of Christ (Luke 15)
Celebrate and rejoice! The dead have been reborn. The
lost have been found. Rejoice and celebrate new life in
our God!

Response to the Word (1 Corinthians 5)
In a world of death and alienation,
we have been remade into a community
of reconciliation.
> **We will proclaim this good news**
> **as Christ's ambassadors of hope.**

Rejoice! Throw a party! Welcome the lonely, the lost!
> **We will sing and dance, laugh and celebrate.**
> **We will invite the last and the least.**

New life is a gift from God,
a gift through Jesus the Christ.
> **Thanks be to God!**

THANKSGIVING AND COMMUNION

Invitation to the Offering (Luke 15)
We, who have feasted on the gift of God's gracious love,
are invited to throw a feast for the prodigals of our world.
Come! Bring your greatest gifts, your richest jewels, your
most scrumptious food! Offer God your very best, for God
has given us the very best in Christ Jesus!

Offering Prayer (Luke 15)
Mother Father God,
> we are poor and lowly, rich and blessed,
> > gifted and graced, downtrodden and unsure;
> we come as we are, offering you all that we have
> > and all that we are.

In Christ Jesus,
> we are reconciled to you,
> made new by your grace,
> > and gifted by your love.

Use these gifts we bring before you,
> as signs of your love and grace in the world.

SENDING FORTH

Benediction (Luke 15)
We, who were lost,
    have been found.
We, who were dead,
    have been given new life.
Go into the world,
    rejoicing that God has welcomed us home.
Go with God's blessing
    to share that welcome with all!

CONTEMPORARY OPTIONS

Contemporary Gathering Words (Luke 15)
Let us worship and celebrate!
Many here were lost,
    but are now found.
Many here were once far away,
    but Christ Jesus has brought them near.
Many here were once dead,
    but are alive again through God's love!
Let us worship and celebrate indeed!

Praise Sentences (Psalm 32, 2 Corinthians 5)
Be glad! Rejoice!
In Christ, we are new, refreshed in love!
    Be glad! Rejoice!

MARCH 21, 2010

Fifth Sunday in Lent

Mary Petrina Boyd

COLOR

Purple

SCRIPTURE READINGS

Isaiah 43:16-21; Psalm 126; Philippians 3:4b-14; John 12:1-8

THEME IDEAS

These scriptures speak not of scarcity, but abundance. The God of the Exodus, who brought the people through the waters of the Red Sea, is about to do something new—something that will surpass God's mighty acts of the past, for now God brings the people home from exile. The abundance of God's caring overflows so that even the wild animals rejoice. Even in the midst of sadness and tears, there is the expectation that joy will abound. Paul finds that the abundance of Jesus Christ surpasses all that he has lost, and looks to the future with hope. The day before Jesus enters Jerusalem, where he will suffer and die, Mary extravagantly anoints Jesus with costly perfume. In this act, she gives of herself to honor him.

INVITATION AND GATHERING

Call to Worship (Isaiah 43, Psalm 126)
God is about to do a new thing!
Do you not see it?
Where should we look?
Now it springs forth.
Do you not sense it?
There is water in the desert.
There are roads in the wilderness.
God is doing something new.
God is doing something wonderful.
We are God's people.
We rejoice in our God.

Opening Prayer (Isaiah 43, John 12)
God of abundant love,
    open our hearts to your gifts.
Free us from our fears and doubts.
Give us generous hearts,
    that we may pour out all that we have
        in service to you.
Teach us to live with expectant joy,
    as we anticipate your transforming grace. Amen.

PROCLAMATION AND RESPONSE

Prayer of Confession (Isaiah 43, Psalm 126, John 12)
Steadfast God,
    throughout the ages
        you have cared for your people.
You lead us through the wilderness of despair
    into a land flowing with joy and hope.
You transform our tears into laughter,
    our sorrow into joy.
Yet we fail to trust you—
    our fears overwhelm us,
    our tears drown our hope.

Afraid of the future,
    we cling to memories of the past.
Forgive us, O God—
    when we criticize others,
    when we are afraid of tomorrow,
    when we lose hope in your goodness.
Give us generous spirits,
    that we may anticipate tomorrow
        with trust in your goodness
        and your steadfast love. Amen.

Words of Assurance (Isaiah 43, Psalm 126)
God is doing a new thing:
    transforming our fears into courage,
    our tears into joy,
    our worries into generosity.
We are God's people—
    a people blessed by divine forgiveness
    and abundant love.

Passing the Peace of Christ (Philippians 3)
The greatest thing we have is the love of God in Christ.
Such love is a precious gift, a rare treasure. Share this gift
as you offer one another the peace of Christ.

Response to the Word (Isaiah 43, John 12)
Loving God, you have cared for us all our lives.
Give us eyes to see your vision for the world.
Give us love to pour out your passion for others.
Give us courage to follow you to a future
    grounded in healing and hope. Amen.

THANKSGIVING AND COMMUNION

Invitation to the Offering (Isaiah 43, John 12)
God offers us life abundant. Like water in the desert or
roads in the wilderness, God's gifts bless the dry and fallow places of our lives. Let us pour out your love and gratitude, as we present our offerings to God.

63

Offering Prayer (Philippians 3)
Generous God,
> in Jesus Christ
>> we have found our true treasure.
Grateful for the faith we have found,
> we bring our gifts
>> in answer to your call
>>> to live in righteousness.
Through our giving,
> draw us into a deeper understanding
>> of your love. Amen.

Invitation to Communion (John 12)
Jesus often shared a meal with those he loved.
One night, when Mary, Martha,
> and Lazarus served him,
>> Mary poured out her rich gift
>> and anointed his head with oil.
She marked him as the Messiah,
> the hope of the world.
Mary responded to his love, giving all she had.
Come then to this table.
It is set with bread and wine.
God's people gather around it.
Jesus again shares a meal with those he loves.

SENDING FORTH

Benediction (Psalm 126)
Go forth with shouts of joy.
> **Tell of God's great deeds!**
Go forth with shouts of joy.
> **Tell the good news of God's love!**

CONTEMPORARY OPTIONS

Contemporary Gathering Words (Isaiah 43)
Something new is happening.
> **It's never happened before!**

God is doing it.
God is doing a new thing.
Are you ready?
We're ready!
God is doing something new.
We're ready to see what it is!

Praise Sentences (Psalm 126)
Our mouths are filled with laughter!
We rejoice in God's love.
Our tongues proclaim our joy!
We praise God's goodness.

MARCH 28, 2010

Palm/Passion Sunday
Bryan Schneider-Thomas

COLOR
Purple

PALM SUNDAY READINGS
Psalm 118:1-2, 19-29; Luke 19:28-40

PASSION SUNDAY READINGS
Isaiah 50:4-9a; Psalm 31:9-16; Philippians 2:5-11;
Luke 22:14–23:56 or Luke 23:1-49

THEME IDEAS
Palm/Passion Sunday offers the choice of focusing on the
triumphal entry of Jesus into Jerusalem or on the entire
passion story. In recent years, the trend has been to use
the entire passion story. This often means that the story of
the triumphal entry is ignored or underplayed. These
liturgies will focus on the themes present in the triumphal
entry, acknowledging the tension of celebrating this joyful
occasion with the knowledge of what comes next. This
presents the opportunity to ask, What is so *good* about the
passion of Christ? If you desire a liturgy that encompasses
the entire passion story, you may wish to draw elements
from Holy Thursday and Good Friday or from previous
years of *The Abingdon Worship Annual*.

INVITATION AND GATHERING

Call to Worship (Palm Sunday)

Honor.
Honor and praise.
Honor, praise, and glory.
Honor, praise, and glory are yours
Almighty God, now and forever.
In celebration, we join the crowds of old,
waving branches, giving honor to the Messiah.
Yet, our celebration is bittersweet,
for our story doesn't end here.
We know the pain of what lies ahead.
Today anticipates the rest of the story—
a story of betrayal and death,
a story of hope and resurrection.

Opening Prayer (Psalm 118, Luke 19)

Save us Lord!
Hosanna!
Praise the Lord!
Alleluia!
To you who triumphed over death,
we sing our praise.
Your steadfast love endures forever.
As we face your death
and recall the week of your suffering,
may we do so with a joy
that anticipates the celebration
of your resurrection;
may we do so with the confidence
to turn to you
in both life and death. Amen.

PROCLAMATION AND RESPONSE

Prayer of Confession (Luke 19)

Lord Jesus,
we are a fickle people,
quick to turn away.

We are quick to flock to you when all is well,
  but we are prone to scatter
    when there is opposition or criticism.
Too often we have kept silent before you,
  afraid to proclaim your praise.
It is easy to join the crowd
  as you ride triumphantly into Jerusalem—
    singing our joys and expectations,
    dancing our hopes and dreams.
It is far more difficult to stand by you
  as the crowd cries for your crucifixion.
Forgive our weakness
  when we turn away.
Strengthen us for the journey ahead
  as we relive your suffering and death,
    that we might stay beside you to the end.
Give us the courage to shout our hosannas,
  not only today, but each and every day. Amen.

Words of Assurance (Psalm 118)
The Lord is our strength and might.
Jesus is our salvation.
  In Jesus our sins are forgiven.
In Jesus our cries are answered,
our salvation is at hand.
  Blessed be the name of the Lord.

Passing the Peace of Christ (Psalm 118)
This is the day that the Lord has made.
  Let us rejoice and be glad in it.
May the peace of Christ fill you this day.
  Christ is the source of our joy and gladness.
Please share a joyful sign of Christ's peace
with those near you.

Response to the Word (Psalm 118, Luke 19)
Blessed is the one who comes in the name
of the Lord.
  Jesus Christ, Son of God, Word made flesh.

Peace in heaven and glory in the highest heaven!
**Open your eyes to see the kingdom
God is creating in our midst.**

THANKSGIVING AND COMMUNION

Invitation to the Offering (Luke 19)
Join in the chorus! Give honor to Jesus Christ and bring
your offering of praise to him. Rejoice in the coming of
our Lord. Lay your treasures at his feet.

Offering Prayer
What can we offer
that you have not already offered us?
What can we do
that you have not already done for us?
Lord Jesus Christ,
in your gifts to us,
you have provided us the way
to live and serve you.
In both your triumph and your suffering,
you deserve our praise.
Through the gifts we now offer,
we express our longing to serve
and to follow wherever you go. Amen.

SENDING FORTH

Benediction (Palm Sunday)
Passing from joy into sorrow and on to elation,
we come to Christ this holy week.
Today is only a part of the story.
**Jesus' triumph leads to his death,
his death to his resurrection.**
May the journey of this week lead you
into the fullness of Christ's love.

CONTEMPORARY OPTIONS

Contemporary Gathering Words (Psalm 118)

Shout out! Don't keep silent.
    God's steadfast love endures forever!
Let the children say:
    God's steadfast love endures forever!
Let the elderly say:
    God's steadfast love endures forever!
Let the women say:
    God's steadfast love endures forever!
Let the men say:
    God's steadfast love endures forever!
Let all who believe say:
    God's steadfast love endures forever!

Praise Sentences (Psalm 118, Luke 19)

Blessed is the one who comes
in the name of the Lord!
    Blessed is the one who comes
    for us all!
Peace in heaven.
    Peace on earth.
And glory in the highest heaven!
    Glory always to Jesus!
Blessed is the one who comes
in the name of the Lord!

APRIL 1, 2010

Holy Thursday

B. J. Beu

COLOR

Purple

SCRIPTURE READINGS

Exodus 12:1-4 (5-10), 11-14; Psalm 116:1-4, 12-19;
1 Corinthians 11:23-26; John 13:1-17, 31b-35

THEME IDEAS

This service is a time of solemn reflection on Jesus' last
night with his disciples. As we remember Christ's gift of
love to us all, we are invited to listen to scripture, share in
Holy Communion and a footwashing ceremony, and sing
the songs of our faith. Jesus becomes a servant to his followers—the ones who betrayed him, denied him, and ran
away in the face of peril. Jesus is an example of faithful
living in an age of unfaithfulness. The footwashing ceremony depicts the depth of Jesus' love for us and offers us
a glimpse of true servanthood. How can we fail to live up
to his example?

INVITATION AND GATHERING

Call to Worship (Psalm 34, John 13)
Our souls hunger for food that satisfies.
Taste and see that the Lord is good!

Our souls are dry and parched from thirst.
Taste and see that the Lord is good!
Our souls long for the bread of heaven.
Taste and see that the Lord is good!
Our souls yearn for the cup of salvation.
Taste and see that the Lord is good!
Let us worship Christ, who invites us to his table.

Opening Prayer (Psalm 116, John 13)
Holy Servant,
　　from the depth of your great love,
　　　　you wash us clean
　　　　　　in the waters of life;
　　from the center of your compassion,
　　　　you satisfy our thirst
　　　　　　with the cup of salvation.
We offer our praise and thanksgiving,
　　as we turn to you once again
　　　　to learn the true meaning
　　　　　　of selfless giving and servanthood.

PROCLAMATION AND RESPONSE

Prayer of Confession (Psalm 116, John 13)
Merciful God,
　　the story of the Passover
　　　　seems so far removed from our lives,
　　yet our need for salvation
　　　　is as great as the ancient Hebrews'.
Forgive us when we feel entitled to be served,
　　while ignoring your call to servanthood.
Forgive us when we feel that love is due us,
　　while denying the love we owe others.
Move us with your generosity
　　and inspire us with your example.
We ask this in the name of your Son,
　　who nourishes us with the bread of heaven
　　　　and enlivens us with the cup of salvation.
Amen.

Words of Assurance (John 13)

Just as Jesus washed the feet
of the one he knew would betray him,
Jesus is here to cleanse us from our sins
and bathe us in the waters of salvation.

Response to the Word (John 13)

We have heard your commandment to love one another as
you have loved us. May our lives display this love every
waking moment, and may the world know that we are
your disciples through our care for one another.

THANKSGIVING AND COMMUNION

Invitation to Footwashing (John 13)

Loving Christ,
on that night long ago
you knew that your hour had come;
you knew what lay ahead of you.
Though your disciples loved and followed you,
they would all fail you—
one would deny you
and one would betray you.
Yet you got on your knees,
and without judgment or resentment,
you washed their feet as a servant—
even the feet of your betrayer.
We have also loved and followed you,
and we have also failed you.
We cannot comprehend the love that heals us,
the love that completes us,
the love that sets us free.
Through this footwashing ceremony,
may we dedicate ourselves
to follow your example
and be servants of all. Amen.

Invitation to Communion (Psalm 34, John 13)

Come and eat, all who are broken;
this is the bread of life, which makes us whole.
We are made one and whole
as we eat from the bread of life.
Come and drink, all who thirst;
this is the cup of salvation, the cup of God's blessing.
We are made one with God
as we drink from the cup of salvation.
Come! Let us eat at Christ's table
in anticipation of the heavenly banquet
that we will share with all God's people.
Taste and see that the Lord is good.

Offering Prayer (Luke 4)

Loving Servant,
  you feed our spiritual hunger
    with the bread of life;
  you satisfy our holy thirst
    with the cup of salvation.
We return thanks for washing our feet
  and for bringing us into full fellowship
    with you and all God's people.
We offer you our very selves,
  that we may fulfill your law of love. Amen.

SENDING FORTH

Benediction (Psalm 116, John 13)

Christ's love has washed us clean.
Christ has chosen us as his own.
Christ's love has fed us with the bread of life
and nourished us with the cup of salvation.
Christ has brought us the gift
of God's heavenly banquet.
Christ's love has brought us the gift
of God's kingdom.
Christ has sealed us in his love.

CONTEMPORARY OPTIONS

Contemporary Gathering Words (John 13)

Christ calls us to love each other.
They will know we are Christians by our love!
Christ calls us to serve each other.
They will know we are Christians by our love!
Christ calls us to lift each other up.
They will know we are Christians by our love!
Christ calls us to share God's love with all.
They will know we are Christians by our love!

Praise Sentences (Psalm 116, John 13)

Wash freely in the waters of salvation.
Give thanksgiving and praise to our God!
Eat freely of the bread of heaven.
Give thanksgiving and praise to our God!
Drink freely of the cup of salvation.
Give thanksgiving and praise to our God!

APRIL 2, 2010

Good Friday

Erik J. Alsgaard

COLOR

Black or none

SCRIPTURE READINGS

Isaiah 52:13–53:12; Psalm 22; Hebrews 10:16-25;
John 18:1–19:42

THEME IDEAS

Somber is the mood for Good Friday, and the Scripture
readings reflect that tone. We hear again the story of Jesus'
betrayal, his being handed over to Pilate, his death on the
cross, and his burial in the tomb. What is the purpose of
Jesus' death? And why do we commemorate this day and
call it "Good"? Isaiah and Hebrews speak of the affliction
of the suffering servant for our transgressions and our iniquities. Through the death of Jesus, our days are pro-
longed, our hopes answered. And in Psalm 22, we find
that, even when we feel forsaken, God is still God; God
has a plan; God is still to be praised.

INVITATION AND GATHERING

Call to Worship (Psalm 22)
O Lord, do not forsake me.
Draw near me, O God!
O Lord, from the pit of my distress,

I cry out to you for help.
Draw near me, O God!
Others mock me for my faith, saying,
"Faith is for the weak!"
Draw near me, O God!
Yet I know that from my birth
you have been with me, O God.
You have always been there!
Even in the midst of deepest despair,
I will sing your praises, O God.
In the midst of the congregation,
I will praise you.
Even today, I will praise you!

Opening Prayer (Psalm 22)
There are times when we feel
you have forsaken us, Lord—
times when we feel alone, betrayed,
beaten, and scorned.
Though our ancestors put their faith in you,
worshiped you, and trusted you,
today we're not so sure.
Many doubts creep into our thoughts—
our cries and prayers seem to go unheard;
we wonder how you could allow your own Son
to be whipped and nailed to a cross to die.
Our unbelief is like the mouth of a lion.
Our fears and doubt are like the horns of the wild ox.
Come to us, O God, and save us.
Help our unbelief,
that we may be an example
for future generations to follow—
examples of faith, praise, and worship. Amen.

PROCLAMATION AND RESPONSE

Prayer of Confession (Psalm 22, Hebrews 10)
We have pierced the sides
of our brothers and sisters, O God,

11

with the arrows of bigotry, hatred,
    neglect, and gossip.
Our bones are out of joint with sin—
    we stumble around, unable to walk in love
    with you and with our neighbors.
Heal us, we pray.
Forgive our sins
    that we pour out to you like water.
Wash us clean
    through the sacrifice of our Lord, Jesus Christ,
    that we may be a redeemed people,
        marked by your love and mercy.
In Jesus' name we pray. Amen.

Assurance of Pardon (Hebrews 10)
It is through Christ's death that our sins
are taken upon the cross. Because of his death,
we have forgiveness of sin. As a forgiven people,
your sins and misdeeds are remembered no more.
In the name of Jesus Christ,
your sins are forgiven!

Response to the Word (Hebrews 10)
We confess, O God,
    that on this day called "Good"
    our hope is diminished.
We've heard again the story
    of your Son's arrest, betrayal, trial, and death,
    and though we know the end of the story,
    we get stuck in our own Good Fridays.
Help us live without wavering
    in the hope of Jesus Christ,
        for your promises never fail.
Your promises never, ever fail. Amen!

THANKSGIVING AND COMMUNION

Invitation to the Offering (John 10)
Christ offered his life that we might no longer fear death.
In response to that incredible sacrifice, let us now offer ourselves back to God as we collect our tithes and offerings.

Offering Prayer (John 10)
O God,
    receive our tithes, our gifts, and our offerings.
Though they pale in comparison
    to what you have done for us
        in the life and death of your Son,
    we pray that through the power
        of your Holy Spirit,
        these gifts will be multiplied many times;
    we pray that your kingdom will come
        one step closer on this earth. Amen.

SENDING FORTH

(A benediction is optional on Good Friday. When we move too quickly from the pain of the cross to the miracle of Easter, we lose the power of Holy Saturday, a day of utter loss and despair. Without this day to lie fallow, without this time to experience the depth of our loss, Easter is robbed of its true joy.)

Benediction (John 10)
The betrayal, suffering, pain, and death of Jesus
    is a powerful reminder of his humanity.
We have heard the story once more,
    and again it has pierced our hearts and our spirit.
Go now into a world that would have you believe
    that death is the final answer,
    that pain and suffering are the only way.
(Optional ending)
Go now, knowing that today is Friday,
    but that Sunday is coming.

CONTEMPORARY OPTIONS

Contemporary Gathering Words (Psalm 22)

Full of sin and shame,
commit your cause to the Lord.
Forsaken, mocked, cast out, and broken,
commit your cause to the Lord.
Anxious, depressed, and short-tempered,
commit your cause to the Lord.
Surrounded by enemies, crushed by pain,
commit your cause to the Lord.
God has not forsaken you or me!
We commit our cause to the Lord!

Praise Sentences (Isaiah 53)

Christ has taken on our iniquities.
He has borne our sin.
He has made new life our hope!
Christ poured himself out to the point of death.
Greatly to be praised is the Lamb of God!

APRIL 4, 2010

Easter Sunday
Marcia McFee

COLOR
White

SCRIPTURE READINGS
Acts 10:34-43; Psalm 118:1-2, 14-24; 1 Corinthians 15:19-26; John 20:1-18 (or Luke 24:1-12)

THEME IDEAS
The scriptures point to the best news of the Christian year: through the resurrection of Christ, we too shall live! In light of this news, we are called to live fully and deeply, and we are called to proclaim our joy from the rooftops. This is a day of singing with passion, celebrating with fervor, and sharing God's goodness with all people. In Acts 10, we are reminded that we are witnesses to God's forgiveness and acceptance every time we eat and drink with the risen Christ. As his friends around the table, we are to testify as Jesus did, telling the good news of peace while doing good and offering life and healing in his name. Providing an opportunity in worship for people to share their own experiences of "resurrection" gives flesh to Mary's words, "I have seen the Lord!"

INVITATION AND GATHERING

Call to Worship (Psalm 118)

(After reading John 20:1-18, bells or chimes begin to peal.)
God is good!
All the time!
And all the time!
God is good!
Give thanks to the Lord, for God is good.
Let all the people proclaim,
"God's steadfast love endures forever!"
God's steadfast love endures forever!
The Lord is my strength, my song, and my salvation!
Shouts of joy resound in the tents of the righteous!
God's steadfast love endures forever!
The Lord's right hand has done mighty things!
We will not die but live.
We will proclaim what the Lord has done.
We enter the gates of the Lord and give thanks,
for this is the day the Lord has made!
Let us rejoice and be glad in it!

Opening Prayer (Acts 10)

Holy and Living God,
like a tomb's darkness that gives way to light,
open us this day to newness of life;
open us to your love, to your acceptance,
to your forgiveness, to your peace;
open us to one another,
and to the possibilities
you have in store for us.
Give us hope for the future
and a passion for life here and now.
We pray in the name
of the One who destroyed death,
Jesus Christ, our Savior. Amen.

PROCLAMATION AND RESPONSE

Prayer for Illumination

Risen One,
> with Mary Magdalene,
> help us recognize you this day
>> as we hear your word and feast together.

You are "Rabboni," our Teacher, our Guide.

Come speak to us,
> that we might be messengers of your love
> and doers of your word. Amen.

Response to the Word

(People may be offered a time to proclaim resurrection experiences in their lives, either to the whole congregation or to someone near them. Alternately, consider writing professions of faith on paper flowers that people can attach to a "flowering cross.")

Christ the Lord is risen today!
Christ is risen indeed!
(B. J. Beu)

THANKSGIVING AND COMMUNION

Offering Prayer (1 Corinthians 15)

Generous God,
> we offer these gifts
>> as our testimony to your glory
>> and as our commitment
>>> as your disciples.

Bless our gifts to your work in the world
> and to your reign here on earth.

Through your blessing of our gifts,
> may death be destroyed
> and hope fill all of creation. Amen.

Invitation to Communion (Acts 10)

As we come to this table with the risen Jesus, we are witnesses to the resurrection! Let us forsake all that holds us back from this joy as we offer our confession.

Communion Prayer (Acts 10)

Jesus our Host,
    we yearn for your Communion;
    we yearn for the hope of new life;
    we yearn to meet you here.
And yet, despite your invitation,
    we find ourselves stumbling on our way.
Forgive us.
Hear now in silence
    the confessions of your people.
(Silence)

Words of Assurance (Acts 10:43)

Hear the good news!
"All the prophets testify about him
that everyone who believes in him
receives forgiveness of sins through his name!"
In the name of the risen Christ, you are forgiven!
In the name of the risen Christ,
you are forgiven! Glory to God!
Amen.

Passing the Peace of Christ

As forgiven, freed, and risen people, testify to the joy of
resurrection as you pass the peace of Christ.

The Great Thanksgiving

The Lord is with you!
And also with you!
Lift up your voices to speak of this great love!
We lift them up in joyful acclamation!
It is right and a good and joyful thing,
    always and everywhere, to give thanks to you,
    Living God.
Time after time, you draw us here to inspire us,
    feed us, and save us.
Especially when our love fails, you are here,
    steadfast and true.
You created this world and called it good.

You created us to proclaim your good to all.
And so we raise our voices in praise:
(Sung Sanctus or a musical setting of Psalm 118)
We remember the life and ministry of Jesus:
    how he healed the sick,
    fed the hungry,
    ate with sinners,
    and preached forgiveness and peace.
It was at this table that he issued the invitation:
    to gather together,
    to share together,
    to remember together,
    and to go and do likewise in the world.
(Words of Institution)
And so, on this day of resurrection,
we raise our voices to proclaim this timeless truth:
    Christ has died. Christ is risen!
    Christ will come again!
Pour out your Holy Spirit on us, your people,
    and on these gifts of bread and cup.
Make us lovers and tellers of your word.
Make us healers and bestowers of your grace.
And make us one body in Jesus Christ.
All glory and honor is yours, Almighty God,
    now and for all time!
    Amen.

SENDING FORTH

Benediction
We have seen the Lord this day!
Now go into the world to spread this good news.
God is good!
    All the time!
And all the time!
    God is good!

May you be blessed and may you be a blessing,
in the name of the Creator, Redeemer, and Sustainer.
Amen.

CONTEMPORARY OPTIONS

Contemporary Gathering Words (John 20)
Open us, O God, like tombs
giving way to your light.
Open us, O God...
to your possibilities,
to your word,
to your surprises,
to your love,
to your grace,
to your risen presence.

Praise Sentences (Psalm 118)
God is good!
All the time!
And all the time!
God is good!
Give thanks to the Lord, for God is good.
God's love endures forever.
Let all people shout it from the rooftops,
"God's love endures forever!"
God's love endures forever!

APRIL 11, 2010

Second Sunday of Easter

Mary J. Scifres

COLOR
White

SCRIPTURE READINGS
Acts 5:27-32; Psalm 150; Revelation 1:4-8; John 20:19-31

THEME IDEAS
This is a day of praise and proclamation. Praise God with all manner of instruments! Proclaim God's dominion and glory, from the first to the last, the beginning to the end, for God is the Alpha and the Omega of all. In the face of doubt and despair, we—like Thomas before us—fall upon our knees and proclaim, "My Lord and my God!"

INVITATION AND GATHERING

Greeting (Revelation 1)
Grace and peace to you from Christ, who was and is and is to come, ruler of all the earth!
Grace and peace to you from Christ,
who frees us in holy love!

Call to Worship (Psalm 150)
Praise God in the sanctuary!
Praise God in the highest heavens!

Sing of mighty deeds and glorious love!
**Sing of amazing greatness
and abundant grace!**
Bang on your drums!
Crash the cymbals!
**Make melody with flutes
and strings and pipes!**
Celebrate with laughter and dancing,
for Christ is alive!
**Let everything that breathes praise the Lord,
for Christ is risen indeed!**

Opening Prayer (Revelation 1, John 20)
Alpha and Omega, our Beginning and End,
we come to you this day
with praise on our lips
and joy in our hearts.
We come to you
with doubt in our minds
and despair in our bones.
From all sorts of places
and with all manner of thoughts,
we come into your presence
to offer you worship and praise.
Breathe upon us with your Spirit,
that we may sense the peace and the glory
of your presence with us.

PROCLAMATION AND RESPONSE

Prayer of Confession (John 20)
Risen Christ,
you know our deepest secrets;
you know our fear-filled doubts;
you know our darkest hours.
Breathe strength and faith into us
in our moments of secret fear.

Grant us the grace
to know your presence
and to trust your promises.
Reclaim us as your disciples.
Reconcile us with your love,
that we may be one with you
and one with each other.
In your holy name, we pray. Amen.

Words of Assurance (Acts 5)

God has exalted the risen Christ
that we might have forgiveness of sins.
We are witnesses to these things.
Rejoice and sing praise to God,
for in Christ, we are forgiven.
In Christ, we are forgiven indeed!

Passing the Peace of Christ (John 20)

As forgiven and reconciled children of God,
let us celebrate Christ's presence
by greeting one another in peace and love.
Peace be with you.
And also with you.

Response to the Word (John 20)

Peace be with you.
And also with you!
Receive the Spirit, the breath of God!
**May the Spirit breathe upon us
and within us.**
For Christ sends us to love and to serve.
**May we move forward in faith,
in the strength of God's Spirit.**

THANKSGIVING AND COMMUNION

Invitation to the Offering (Psalm 150)

Let everything that has breath praise the Lord! Let everyone who has gifts praise the Lord! Let all who are blessed

praise the Lord! May we offer our praise and our gratitude as we share our gifts and our blessings with a world
in need.

Offering Prayer (John 20)

Risen Christ,
>
> you proclaim us blessed
> when we believe
> even where we have not seen.

Bless these gifts, given in faith and hope,
> that they may be visible reminders
> of your presence in the world.

May those who cannot believe without seeing,
> see in these gifts your loving grace—
> a grace present and available to all. Amen.

SENDING FORTH

Benediction (Revelation 1, John 20)

Look! Christ is coming with the clouds!
Believe! Christ is risen!
Go! Share the good news!

CONTEMPORARY OPTIONS

Contemporary Gathering Words (John 20)

The doors that were closed are now open!
The tomb that was sealed is flung wide!
Christ who was dead is alive!
See! Christ is with us now!

Praise Sentences (Psalm 150)

Praise God with song and dance!
Praise God with song and dance!
Praise God with strings and pipe!
Praise God with strings and pipe!
Let everything that breathes praise the Lord!
Let everything that breathes praise the Lord!

APRIL 18, 2010

Third Sunday of Easter /
Native American Awareness Sunday
B. J. Beu

COLOR
White

SCRIPTURE READINGS
Acts 9:1-6 (7-20); Psalm 30; Revelation 5:11-14; John 21:1-19

THEME IDEAS
God's love rescues us in many ways. On the road to Damascus, Saul is rescued from himself—from his desire to persecute the fledgling Christian community to the detriment of his soul. The psalmist extols God's power to heal us and save us from our foes. The book of Revelation rejoices in the Lamb, who takes away the sins of the world. And in the Gospel of John, Jesus takes away the shame of Peter's three public denials by requiring three public declarations of his love. Love rescues us and calls us to action: Saul to proclaim the gospel; Peter to feed his masters' sheep. Just as God rescues us from the pit, God calls us to follow Jesus.

INVITATION AND GATHERING

Call to Worship (Acts 9, Psalm 30)
Great winds drive us across the sky,
opening our hearts to the promise of each day.

The Spirit moves in our lives,
turning our mourning into dancing.
Weeping may last the night,
but joy comes with the morning.
Great winds drive us across the sky,
opening our hearts to the promise of each day.

Opening Prayer (Acts 9, John 21)
Lord of Life,
    you meet us on the road
        and shake the very foundations
            of our lives.
Remove the scales from our eyes,
    that we may see your Spirit
        in beliefs foreign to our own;
    that we may see the sheep of your pasture
        in every culture we encounter;
    that we may see the dawn of your love,
        in every morning's sunrise.
Fill us with your Spirit,
    that we may love one another
        as our shepherd has loved us. Amen.

PROCLAMATION AND RESPONSE

Prayer of Confession (Acts 9, John 21)
Merciful God,
    in our ignorance:
        we have trampled upon
            the native peoples of this land;
        we have felt ourselves spiritually superior,
            failing to recognize your presence
                in their midst.
Like Saul before us,
    we have sought to root out the error in others,
    while failing to see the faults in ourselves.

Rescue us when we stray,
   and renew our desire,
      not only to declare our love for you,
      but to live that love in our care for others.

Words of Assurance (Psalm 30)
God is gracious. The Lord is our helper.
The time for weeping is over,
   for joy comes with the morning.
Rejoice, people of God.
God's Spirit saves us in every way.

Response to the Word (John 21)
Here and now, Christ asks us:
   "Do you love me? Feed my lambs."
Christ challenges us:
   "Do you love me? Tend my sheep."
Christ calls to us:
   "Do you love me? Feed my sheep."

THANKSGIVING AND COMMUNION

Offering Prayer (Acts 9, Psalm 30, Revelation 5, John 21)
Great Spirit,
   you rescue us from the pit;
   you offer us your very self;
   you free us from delusion.
After a long slumber in ignorance and fear,
   we offer you our gratitude
      for the joy of new life
         that comes in the morning.
Lamb of God,
   accept our gifts
      as signs of our commitment
         to love one another. Amen.

SENDING FORTH

Benediction (Revelation 5, John 21)
The Spirit blows us across the sky,
showing us God's little ones.
The Lamb of God looks on us with love,
calling us to feed God's sheep.
The Spirit leads us into life,
**bringing us the joy that comes
with the morning.**

CONTEMPORARY OPTIONS

*Contemporary Gathering Words or Benediction
(John 21)*
Christ calls us in love: "Feed my lambs."
Great Spirit, lead us in love.
Christ beckons us in hope: "Tend my sheep."
Great Spirit, guide us in hope.
Christ meets us in service: "Feed my sheep."
Great Spirit, free us in service.

Praise Sentences (Psalm 30, Revelation 5)
Sing praises to the Lord.
Give thanks to God's holy name.
Worthy is the Lamb—
all blessing, honor, and glory forever!
Sing praises to the Lord.
Give thanks to God's holy name.

APRIL 25, 2010

Fourth Sunday of Easter / Heritage Sunday

Bill Hoppe

COLOR

White

SCRIPTURE READINGS

Acts 9:36-43; Psalm 23; Revelation 7:9-17; John 10:22-30

THEME IDEAS

It would be easy to focus on the words "the Lord is my shepherd" as the central theme of today's readings. Certainly there is no more beautiful and perfect description of a life lived in harmony with God than Psalm 23. No less important, however, is the passage from Revelation 7, "God will wipe away every tear from their eyes." The Lord is indeed our shepherd, as Jesus explains in John 10. The Good Shepherd cares for the sheep, brings an end to suffering, and fulfills the promise of eternal life as described in Revelation and experienced firsthand by Peter in Acts.

INVITATION AND GATHERING

Call to Worship (Revelation 7)
From every nation, in every language, we cry out:
**"Salvation belongs to our God,
and to the Lamb!"**

Amen! Blessing and glory and wisdom
and thanksgiving!
**Honor and power and might be to our God
forever and ever!**
Amen!
Amen!

Opening Prayer (Psalm 23, John 10, Revelation 7)

You are the Good Shepherd, Lord,
we hear your call;
we know your voice;
we follow your paths.
You lead us beside still waters.
You guide us to the springs of life.
You shelter us and restore our souls.
In you we find life everlasting.
We come humbly into your presence this day,
in praise, worship, and adoration.
Our hearts run over
with your unfailing goodness
and never-ending love.
In the name of our Savior, we pray. Amen.

PROCLAMATION AND RESPONSE

Prayer of Confession (Psalm 23, John 10, Revelation 7)

Master, Savior, Shepherd, Messiah—
we know you by many names, Lord.
Your presence fills our lives—
all that we are and all that we have
comes from you;
all that you do declares your love for us.
Yet when trouble comes,
when adversity plagues us,
we wonder where you are;
we even wonder who you are.
How quickly we forget
that you are always with us.

Dispel our gloom and despair.
Change our garments of darkness
    into robes of dazzling light.
Spread your table before us,
    and feed us from your hand.
Lead us in the paths of righteousness,
    for it is in your name that we pray. Amen.

Words of Assurance (Psalm 23, John 10, Revelation 7)
Even in the darkest valley,
    though death's shadow may threaten us,
    we need not fear, for the Lord is with us.
God will comfort and shelter us.
No harm will come to us.
No one can snatch us out of the Lord's hand.
God will wipe away every tear from our eyes.

Passing the Peace of Christ (Acts 9)
As Peter gave his hand to Tabitha in prayer and healing,
so Christ extends a loving hand to us. Share the peace of
Christ with your neighbor. Greet one another in the Lord.

Response to the Word (Psalm 23, John 10, Revelation 7)
We have heard your voice, Lord.
You have spoken to us plainly.
We will follow you
    as you guide us on the right paths.
We will respond to you,
    as you open our hearts and minds
        and fill us with life in all its fullness.
Hear our prayer, Lord,
    in the name of the Savior. Amen.

THANKSGIVING AND COMMUNION

Offering Prayer (John 10)
Gracious and loving God,
    all of your works,
    all that you have done for us,
        testify to your love.

You gave everything
　　to bring us the promise of eternal life.
By the power of the Holy Spirit,
　　may all that we do and all that we are
　　　　testify to your amazing care and compassion.
In gratitude and love,
　　we offer ourselves to you. Amen.

SENDING FORTH

Benediction (Psalm 23, Revelation 7)
　　The Lord is our shepherd; we want for nothing.
　　We hunger and thirst no more.
　　The Lord gives rest and comfort to our souls.
　　God keeps us in perfect peace.
　　The Lord sustains us in the midst of trouble.
　　Our lives overflow with God's love and grace.
　　Goodness and mercy will surely follow us always.
　　And we will dwell in the house of the Lord forever!

CONTEMPORARY OPTIONS

Contemporary Gathering Words (Psalm 23, John 10, Revelation 7)
　　We come to worship before God's throne.
　　The Lamb is our Good Shepherd.
　　We are the sheep of his pasture.
　　The Lamb leads the flock in safety.
　　The Shepherd gives his life for the sheep.
　　All praise to God and to the Lamb!

Praise Sentences (Revelation 7)
　　Blessing, glory, and honor be yours forever!
　　Amen!
　　Blessing, glory, and honor be yours forever!
　　Amen!

MAY 2, 2010

Fifth Sunday of Easter
Mary Petrina Boyd

COLOR
White

SCRIPTURE READINGS
Acts 11:1-18; Psalm 148; Revelation 21:1-6; John 13:31-35

THEME IDEAS
These scriptures proclaim both the power of God, who creates all that is, and the love of God for all people. Through a vision, God shows Peter that the Gentiles are to be included in the promises of Jesus Christ. The psalmist calls all creation to praise its creator. In Revelation, we hear that God's home is among people and we receive the promise that grief will be no more. In John's Gospel, Jesus gives his disciples the commandment to love one another.

INVITATION AND GATHERING

Call to Worship (Psalm 148)
Praise the Lord!
> **Praise the Lord from the heavens.**
> **Praise God from the heights!**
Praise the Lord, you angels.
Sing praise, you heavenly host!
> **Praise the Lord, O sun and moon.**
> **Join in song, O shining stars!**

99

Praise the Lord, snow and rain.
Blow loud, wind and storm!
Praise the Lord, O trees.
Dance with joy, O birds!
Praise the Lord, women and men.
Rejoice, children and rulers!
Praise the Lord, weak and strong.
Sing for joy, timid and bold!
Praise the Lord, mothers and aunts.
Give praise, grandfathers and cousins!
Let all creation praise God's name!
Praise the Lord!

Opening Prayer (Revelation 22, John 13)
Alpha and Omega,
    you make your home with us,
    you dry our tears and quench our thirst,
    you are the tender love
        that welcomes all people.
Like a mother,
    you nurture your children,
    giving them life,
    teaching them to love.
Come and dwell among us,
    and make all things new. Amen.

PROCLAMATION AND RESPONSE

Prayer of Confession (Acts 11, John 13)
God of all people,
    our hearts are too narrow,
    our perspectives are too small.
We reject those who are not like us—
    those with different political opinions,
    those who struggle with mental illness,
    those who disagree with us.
We forget that all are your beloved children,
    and neglect your call to love one another.

Forgive us, O God,
for the many ways we have failed
to be a people known by our love.
Show us how to be more caring.
Teach us how to love one another,
and make us faithful disciples. Amen.

Words of Assurance (Acts 11, Revelation 21)
God dwells among us,
giving to all who believe
the repentance that leads to life.
Rejoice in the Lord,
for we are a forgiven people.

Passing the Peace of Christ (Acts 11)
Peter discovered that all are included in God's welcome.
Share this welcome with those around you. May Christ's
peace be with us all.

Response to the Word (Acts 11)
Loving God,
we are often upset
by people who are not like us—
those who think differently,
those who act differently,
those who speak differently.
Our parched hearts are thirsty for your love.
Our dry spirits are thirsty for your waters of life.
Pour your love over us and transform us,
that we may embrace all people as your own. Amen.

THANKSGIVING AND COMMUNION

Invitation to the Offering (Acts 11, John 13)
God has given us the gift of faith. Through this gift we
see all people as God's children. Respond to God's generous love, that we may love one another as God has
loved us. Let us share this love as we bring our tithes and
offerings.

Offering Prayer (John 13)
Loving God,
you have given us the task
to love one another.
May the gifts we offer
bring love and life to others.
May the love we share
bring hope to a world
that has forgotten how to love. Amen.

Invitation to Communion (Acts 11, Revelation 21)
As God revealed to Peter, the table is open to all. Jesus offers gifts of bread and wine to all who believe. When we gather here, we have a glimpse of the holy city, where God is at work making all things new. The one who is the Alpha and the Omega invites us to the banquet.

SENDING FORTH

Benediction (John 13)
Jesus gave a new commandment:
to love one another.
Because Jesus loves us,
we should love one another.
Go forth to serve.
Go forth to love.
We go with God's love and blessing.

CONTEMPORARY OPTIONS

Contemporary Gathering Words (Psalm 99)
Praise the Lord, all you people!
Praise the Lord, all you men,
women, and children!
Praise the Lord, all you citizens of God!
Praise the Lord, all you young
and old alike!

Praise the Lord, all you creatures!
**Praise the Lord, all you sea monsters
and fish of the deep!**
Praise the Lord, all you lands!
**Praise the Lord, all you mountains,
forests, and meadows!**
Let everything that is praise the Lord.
Praise the Lord!

Praise Sentences (Revelation 21)
God is the Alpha and the Omega,
the beginning and the end!
God revives us with water from the spring of life.
God makes all things new.
God dwells with us.
Death is no more.
Praise be to God!

MAY 9, 2010

*Sixth Sunday of Easter / Festival of the
Christian Home / Mother's Day*

Mary J. Scifres

COLOR

White

SCRIPTURE READINGS

Acts 16:9-15; Psalm 67; Revelation 21:1-10; 22–22:5;
John 14:23-29

THEME IDEAS

Visions and dreams guide believers through much of the
Easter experience. Jesus paints a picture of a time when
he will be absent, but God's Spirit will become the teacher
and guide. Paul's vision leads him not only to preach, but
also to encounter Lydia. As God opens her heart, Lydia
believes and is baptized with her entire household, becoming one of the key supporters of the early church.
John's vision in Revelation prophesies an even more glorious day when God will bring forth a new heaven and a
new earth.

INVITATION AND GATHERING

Call to Worship (Psalm 67, Revelation 21)
Let us praise our God!
Let us dream mighty dreams!

Let us dream of light for our path!
Let us be light for the world!
Let us praise our God!
Let us dream mighty dreams!

Opening Prayer (Revelation 21, John 14)

Holy Spirit, giver of dreams,
    instill in us your vision
        and hope for new life.
Breathe upon us
    your peace and strength.
Enlighten our minds
    with your wisdom and truth.
Light our way,
    that we may be a light to the nations.
Open our hearts,
    that we may listen and love.

PROCLAMATION AND RESPONSE

Prayer of Confession (Revelation 21, John 14)

God of light and life,
    you know when we lose our way—
        when we walk in darkness,
        when we close our hearts
            to your truth and wisdom,
        when we do not keep your word,
        when we do not love
            as you have taught us to love.
Let your face shine upon us,
    that we may see your love
        shining through our failures.
Be gracious unto us,
    that we may bask in the glow
        of your forgiveness.
Bathe us in the waters of life,
    that we may be born anew
        and shine as children of love.
Amen and amen.

Words of Assurance (John 14)

Hear these words of promise from Jesus our Savior:
"Peace I leave with you;
   my peace I give to you.
I do not give to you as the world gives.
Do not let your hearts be troubled,
   and do not let them be afraid."
Trust these words and receive grace upon grace.
Forgiveness is ours. Thanks be to God!

Passing the Peace of Christ (Revelation 21, John 14)

Forgiven and reconciled to God, let us share signs of light, life, and love with one another. Peace Christ gives to us. Our peace, we now give to one another.

Response to the Word or Prayer of Preparation (Revelation 21, John 14)

God of light and life,
   shine upon us
      with your wisdom and truth.
Open our hearts
   to listen eagerly
      and to love generously.
As you teach us,
   so may we live in your world
      as lights shining with your glory.
May we be like trees of life,
   offering healing to a world in need.

THANKSGIVING AND COMMUNION

Invitation to the Offering (John 14, Acts 16)

As Lydia opened her heart, her home, and even her purse, so may we open ourselves to God and to one another. Let us share our hearts and our gifts with God through Christ's church.

Offering Prayer (Revelation 21)

Receive these gifts,
   and bless them with the power
      of your Holy Spirit.

Transform these gifts and our very lives,
    that through our giving,
      and through our living,
      we may shine like a city upon a hill,
        glowing with the light of your love.
In Christ's name, we pray. Amen.

SENDING FORTH

Benediction (Psalm 67, John 14)
May the God of new life bless you
    and be gracious to you.
May the face of Christ shine upon you.
And may the Spirit of love
    flow within you and through you.

CONTEMPORARY OPTIONS

Contemporary Gathering Words (Acts 16, Revelation 21)
Come to the fountain of life.
Open your hearts to the truths we will hear.
Look upon the glory of God.
God's love is shining upon us even now.

Praise Sentences (Psalm 67)
Let all people praise the Lord.
    Praise be to God!
Let everyone here praise the Lord.
    Praise be to God!

MAY 16, 2010

Ascension Sunday
Ciona Rouse

COLOR
White

SCRIPTURE READINGS
Acts 1:1-11; Psalm 47; Ephesians 1:15-23; Luke 24:44-53

THEME IDEAS
Ascension Sunday is a time to recognize God's glory and rule over the earth. Jesus has been given power and dominion over all things. This Sunday, we can highlight this regal Jesus, our humble King of kings. The music and atmosphere of worship this day should reflect the reign of the ascended Christ over all things. It should also draw us to a place where we recognize that our calling comes from the most high: we must search for the hope to which God has called us.

INVITATION AND GATHERING

Call to Worship (Psalm 47)
Clap your hands! Shout for joy!
Our Lord reigns on the throne of glory!
We open our hearts to the ascended Lord,
who sits on the throne of glory!

Opening Prayer (Ephesians 1)

Lord of Lords,
  illumine our hearts this day,
  that we may feel your glory
    and live into the hope
      to which you have called us. Amen.

PROCLAMATION AND RESPONSE

Prayer of Confession (Luke 24)

O Lord,
  we have not lived our lives
    as kingdom people.
We place our crowns
  on hopelessness, fear,
  and selfishness.
We are ruled by our schedules
  and our need for control.
We make kings of the things we acquire
  and queens of our immediate desires.
We forget that your kingdom
  draws near to us on earth,
    as it is in heaven.
Forgive us, we pray.
Come, Lord,
  and open in us
    the gates of your kingdom. Amen.

Words of Assurance (Luke 24)

The God of our Lord Jesus Christ
blesses us and calls us "kingdom people."
In the name of the reigning Christ,
we are forgiven.
  In the name of the reigning Christ,
  we are forgiven. Glory to God! Amen.

Passing the Peace of Christ (Acts 1)

The glory of God reigns in each of us! Let the peace of Christ
within you greet the peace of Christ in your neighbor.

Response to the Word (Ephesians 1)
The word of God speaks to our hearts.
(Silent reflection)
The word of God speaks to our community.
(Silent reflection)
The word of God speaks to our nation.
(Silent reflection)
The word of God speaks to our world.
(Silent reflection)
May God give us a spirit of wisdom and revelation
as we come to know Christ.
**Lord, help us know the glorious hope
to which you have called us
through your word.**

THANKSGIVING AND COMMUNION

Invitation to the Offering (Luke 24)
Gifted with the grace of God, and clothed with power
from on high, let us now offer ourselves to the building
of God's kingdom.

Offering Prayer (Luke 24)
Bless these gifts, O Lord of all,
that we might worship you with great joy
and serve your people with great love.
In Christ's name, amen.

Invitation to Communion
Come to the table. It's an open feast.
Christ invites us all—
the rich and the poor,
the outcast and the honored.
Come to the gathering of sinners and saints.
Come to this blessed table where Christ reigns.
Come and taste the kingdom of God,
where all are welcome.

Prayer following Communion

Lord, you have given us peace
and blessed us with a taste
of your heavenly banquet.
As we leave your table,
usher us into your kingdom,
now and forever. Amen.

SENDING FORTH

Benediction (Psalm 47)

Clap your hands all you people!
Sing to God with songs of joy!
Go forth praising God, who reigns on high!

CONTEMPORARY OPTIONS

Contemporary Gathering Words (Acts 1, Luke 24)

Christ is lifted up to God.
Christ is lifted up in our hearts.
Christ draws us up to the heights.
Christ draws us up to God.
Let us worship the one
who rose into heaven
to bring us eternal life.
(B. J. Beu)

Praise Sentences (Luke 24)

Christ reigns!
Alleluia!
Christ reigns!
Shout for joy!
Christ reigns!
Alleluia!
Christ reigns forever!
Christ reigns indeed!
(B. J. Beu)

III

MAY 23, 2010

Pentecost Sunday
Laura Jaquith Bartlett

COLOR
Red

SCRIPTURE READINGS
Acts 2:1-21; Psalm 104:24-34, 35b; Romans 8:14-17; John 14:8-17 (25-27)

THEME IDEAS
Despite the good news of the resurrection, the post-Easter disciples were a rather tentative bunch. They had lost their leader. There was dissension all around them. They were understandably afraid, for their friend and teacher had just been executed by the government. Into their already turbulent lives blew the life-changing wind of the Holy Spirit. Yikes! But as promised in John, the Advocate empowers, comforts, encourages, and strengthens the disciples. To claim the same gifts today, we need only give our fears to the Wind, and open our lives to be transformed.

INVITATION AND GATHERING

Gathering Words (John 14)
Even after the resurrection, when the disciples
were weighed down with worry,
> **Jesus assured them that they were not alone:**
> **"The Holy Spirit, whom the Father will send**

in my name, will teach you everything,
and remind you of all that I have said to you."
Even after the resurrection, when the disciples
were burdened by their fears,
Jesus calmed their troubled hearts:
"Do not let your hearts be troubled,
and do not let them be afraid."
Even after the resurrection, when we struggle
with our faith,
Jesus blesses us with comfort and hope:
"Peace I leave with you; my peace
I give to you."
Especially after the resurrection, when our souls
are dry and barren,
the Holy Spirit blows through our lives,
bringing us new life. Alleluia!

Opening Prayer (Acts 2, John 14)
Amazing God,
you call us today,
just as you called the disciples
on the Day of Pentecost.
You challenge and support us,
revealing the brokenness of our communities;
giving us the peace that our world needs.
You point us to the pain of the cross,
and then remind us of the joy of the resurrection.
Transform us, O God,
through the power of your Holy Spirit.
Help us breathe deeply
of the Breath of Life.
Blow through our worship
and change our lives forever. Amen.

PROCLAMATION AND RESPONSE

Prayer of Confession (Acts 2)
Holy Spirit,
we're not sure we're ready

113

for your awesome power
    to blow through our lives;
we're grown comfortable
    with our familiar habits
    and our bland routines;
we're afraid to give up our waking slumber
    and face the truth
        that we do not truly live.
When we cling to our ways
    and the safety of familiar paths,
        wake us up,
        shake us up,
        heat us up,
        and breathe your life into us.
Walk with us, O God,
    and give us the courage
        to follow the way that is lit
        by the fire of your Spirit.
On this Day of Pentecost,
    we pray for the audacity
        to ride the winds of change. Amen.

Words of Assurance (John 14)
Hear these words of Jesus:
    "Peace I leave with you; my peace
    I give to you.... Do not let your hearts
    be troubled, and do not let them be afraid."
In the midst of our fears and doubts,
    the peace of the Holy Spirit will prevail.

Passing the Peace of Christ (John 14)
When Jesus left his disciples, he did not leave them alone.
He promised that the Holy Spirit would be present in their
lives, and he gave them an amazing gift: his peace, the
peace of Christ. Through the Spirit, this gift lives still, and
it is ours to share with others. Turn to those around you
and offer Christ's gift with these words: "The peace of
Christ is yours today!"

Response to the Word (Acts 2, Psalm 104, John 14)
Holy Spirit,
    we are not ready for you,
    but we know that you are ready for us—
        ready to change our lives if we will let you.
Help us prepare
    by setting our hearts on fire with love;
    by blowing away our fears and doubts;
    by tuning our ears to the rich diversity
        of language and culture around the world;
    by opening our eyes to the amazing beauty
        and power of your creation;
    by breathing into us
        the joy and hope of the resurrected Christ,
        in whose name we pray. Amen.

THANKSGIVING AND COMMUNION

Offering Prayer (Acts 2, John 14)
Pentecost God,
    take our hearts and set them on fire.
Take our lives and transform them.
Take our church and resurrect it
    with your life-giving Spirit.
Take our gifts and use them
    for the fulfillment of your vision
    of peace and unity. Amen.

SENDING FORTH

Benediction (Acts 2, Psalm 104, John 14)
The God who made this amazing universe
    is creating you anew every day.
Jesus Christ, the resurrected One,
    offers you peace that never dies.
The Holy Spirit is setting your hearts on fire—
    right here, right now.
Go in peace, and be transformed,
    that you may change the world. Amen.

CONTEMPORARY OPTIONS

Contemporary Gathering Words (Acts 2)

Leader 1: Jesus Christ is alive and with us today!

Leader 2: *(Disbelieving)* What?

Leader 1: Get ready for some excitement: Jesus is right here, right now!

Leader 2: Come on, this is the twenty-first century. We don't believe that kind of thing any-more.

Leader 1: Can't you feel the Spirit? God is ready to change us *today*!

Leader 2: What are you babbling about? We don't feel anything.

Leader 1: It's true! God's Spirit is going to set us on fire today, so get ready.

Leader 2: *(Turning away in disgust)* This is ridiculous. You must be drunk!

All: **It *is* true! The Holy Spirit has set us on fire with the crazy joy of the resurrection. We're ready for God to change us *today*!**

Praise Sentences (Psalm 104)

O Lord, how manifold are your works!
Bless the Lord, O my soul.
Praise the Lord!
Praise the Lord!
Praise the Lord!

MAY 30, 2010

Trinity Sunday / Peace with Justice Sunday

B. J. Beu

COLOR
White

SCRIPTURE READINGS
Proverbs 8:1-4, 22-31; Psalm 8; Romans 5:1-5; John 16:12-15

THEME IDEAS
God takes delight in the human race. During the creation of the inhabited world, Wisdom rejoiced before God, taking delight in the human race. The psalmist marvels that amid the wonders of creation, human beings were created but a little lower than God. Paul boasts of our hope to share in God's glory through the love poured out to us in the Holy Spirit. And John declares that this same Spirit will lead us into all truth. On Trinity Sunday, we celebrate the fullness of God that leads us into the fullness of life.

INVITATION AND GATHERING

Call to Worship (Psalm 8)
O Lord, our God, how majestic is your name
in all the earth!
Your voice causes the sea to roar
and the wind to howl.

You have set your glory above the heavens.
The moon and the stars sing your praises.
What are human beings that you are mindful of us?
Who are we that you care for us?
Yet you have made us a little lower than God.
You have crowned us with glory and honor.
O Lord, our God, how majestic is your name
in all the earth!

Opening Prayer (Proverbs 8, Psalm 8, John 16)
Holy Wisdom, Spirit of Truth,
    we behold your glory in the starry heavens,
        and your wonder in the earth and sea.
Who are we that you care for us so deeply?
Why do you love us so completely?
May we heed your clarion call—
    to lead lives steeped in your wisdom,
        and to take delight in all of your goodness.
Come into our lives and lead us
    into the fullness of your truth,
    that our lives might glorify you
        in all that we say and do. Amen.

PROCLAMATION AND RESPONSE

Prayer of Confession (John 16)
Spirit of Truth,
    we find ourselves unable still
    to bear the things
        you would say to us.
We have trusted our own wisdom,
    turning away from the fullness of truth
        that you alone reveal.
Forgive our inattention,
    and guide us into the sheer delight
        of bearing witness to your glory. Amen.

Assurance of Pardon (Romans 5)
Trust in the Lord, for God's promises are sure.
Hope in the Lord, for God's love

is poured into our hearts through the Holy Spirit.
Through God's live-giving Spirit, we are forgiven. Amen!

Response to the Word (John 16)

As we reflect upon the word of God, may the Spirit of
Truth bring us wisdom, that we might carry the message
of the gospel in our hearts. As we live according to the
word of God, may the Spirit of Truth guide us into all
truth, that we might reflect God's glory.

THANKSGIVING AND COMMUNION

Offering Prayer (Psalm 8)

Sovereign God,
> you have set us as stewards
> over the works of your hands.
May the offerings we bring you this day
> reflect the seriousness of your commission
> to be stewards of your gifts;
> may they be signs of our willingness
> to share joyfully the bounty of your world. Amen.

SENDING FORTH

Benediction (Proverbs 8, Psalm 8, Romans 5, John 16)

Go with the blessings of the Holy Spirit.
God's Spirit leads us into truth.
Go with the blessing of Holy Wisdom.
God's Wisdom is our delight.
Go with the blessing of the Son of God.
God's inheritance fills us with joy.
Go with grace and peace.

CONTEMPORARY OPTIONS

Contemporary Gathering Words (Proverbs 8)

Wisdom rejoices and delights in the Lord!
How can we keep from singing?

Wisdom dances and twirls with joy before God.
How can we keep from dancing?
Wisdom proclaims the glory of God.
How can we keep from rejoicing?
Wisdom rejoices and delights in the Lord!
How can we keep from singing?

Praise Sentences (Proverbs 8, Psalm 8)

God's name is above all names.
Our delight is in the Lord!
The works of God are a wonder to behold.
Our delight is in the Lord!
God fills us with glory.
Our delight is in the Lord!
Praise God's holy name!
Our delight is in the Lord!

JUNE 6, 2010

Second Sunday after Pentecost
Mary J. Scifres

COLOR

Green

SCRIPTURE READINGS

1 Kings 17:8-24; Psalm 146; Galatians 1:11-24; Luke 7:11-17

THEME IDEAS

Miracles of life and hope emerge as the themes of 1 Kings and Luke 7. Elijah transforms an empty jar into an abundant supply of grain, and then raises a child from a death-like illness. Jesus comforts a grieving mother, and then brings her son back from the dead. God's presence is revealed and recognized through these miracles, and both Elijah and Jesus are seen as messengers of the God who watches over widows, and who gives food to the hungry.

INVITATION AND GATHERING

Call to Worship (1 Kings, Psalm 146, Luke 7)
Women and men, young and old,
Christ calls to us: "Arise!"
Sing praise to Christ, who brings forth new life!
Sorrowing and sorrowful, downtrodden and poor,
Christ calls to us: "Arise!"
Sing praise to Christ, who lifts us up.

Families and beloved, lonely and betrayed ones,
Christ calls to us: "Arise!"
Sing praise to Christ, who comforts and cares.
Happy are we whose help is in the Lord.
Blessed are we whose hope is in our God.
With hope and joy, we lift our songs of praise.
Sing praise to God, who lifts us up
and holds us close.

Opening Prayer (1 Kings 17, Psalm 147, Luke 7)

God of help and hope,
pour out the power of your Holy Spirit
on your people gathered here.
Help us recognize the miracle
of your constant presence in our lives.
Lift us up,
that we may rise with new life and new hope
as children of your miracles
and faithful followers of your Son,
Christ Jesus our Lord. Amen.

PROCLAMATION AND RESPONSE

Prayer of Confession (1 Kings 17, Psalm 146, Luke 7)

Ancient One, ever new,
forgive us when we neglect to care
for the widows and the orphans,
the bereaved and the lonely;
forgive us when we fail to be signs
of your miraculous help in the world.
Instill in us the constant hope
and the steadfast faithfulness—
to be your disciples,
to be your messengers,
to be your hands and feet in this world.
(Time of silent reflection)
In the name of the risen Christ,
who brought hope and healing to our world,
we pray. Amen.

Words of Assurance (Psalm 146, Luke 7)
Happy are those whose help is in God,
    the one who made heaven and earth.
Blessed are those whose hope is in Christ,
    the one who keeps faith forever.
In that spirit of faithfulness,
    God in Christ has forgiven us
    and invites us to rise in new life.

Passing the Peace of Christ (Luke 7)
Let us rise together and offer one another signs of Christ's miracles. Let us offer one another messages of life and peace.

Response to the Word (Psalm 146, Galatians 1, Luke 7)
We know that the gospel proclaimed today
is not of human origin.
    May we hear God's word as a revelation
    of Christ's very presence.
We know that God's messengers are never perfect,
be they Paul and Elijah, or preachers and priests.
    May we respond to God's message
    with steadfast faith and conviction,
    perceiving Christ's perfect presence
    even in imperfect people.
Christ calls to us: "Arise!"
We are sent to spread the news:
    Our hope is in Christ the Lord!

THANKSGIVING AND COMMUNION

Invitation to the Offering (1 Kings 17)
Do not be afraid. God's gifts overflow in abundance. Our jars will not fail. Our cups will not empty. Do not be afraid. Give generously as God has given generously to you.

Offering Prayer (1 Kings 17, Luke 7)
Abundant God,
    we thank you for the jars of our lives
        that are constantly being filled.

We offer our gifts to you,
    that others may know
        of your abundance and grace.
Fill the hungry with good things.
Lift up the oppressed.
Watch over the stranger
    and comfort the lonely.
Through our gifts,
    may we do likewise.
In the name of Christ the Comforter, we pray.

The Great Thanksgiving (1 Kings 17, Psalm 146, Luke 7)

The Lord be with you.
And also with you.
Lift up your hearts.
We lift them up to the Lord.
Let us give thanks to the Lord our God.
It is right to give our thanks and praise.
It is right, and a good and joyful thing,
    always and everywhere to give thanks to you,
    Almighty God, creator of heaven and earth.
You formed us in your image
    and breathed into us the breath of life.
You spoke to us through your prophets,
    revealing your love through miracles
    of help and hope.
When we were afraid and alone,
    you walked alongside us
    bringing comfort and kindness.
When we turned away and our love failed,
    your love remained steadfast.
You delivered us from death and despair,
    and made covenants with us time and again.
And so, with your people on earth,
    and all the company of heaven,
    we praise your name
    and join their unending hymn, saying:

Holy, holy, holy Lord,
   God of power and might,
   heaven and earth are full of your glory.
Hosanna in the highest!
Blessed is the one
   who comes in the name of the Lord.
Hosanna in the highest!
Holy are you and blessed is your Son, Jesus Christ.
Your Spirit anointed him
   to execute justice for the oppressed,
   to give food to the hungry,
   to set the prisoner free.
In Christ, you opened the eyes of the blind
   and lifted up those who were bowed down.
You again proclaimed your care of the widow
   and the orphan, the stranger and the bereaved.
Even when facing death, Jesus reached out
   to the grieving and sorrowful,
   to his mother and his beloved disciple,
   even to his betrayer and his denier.
And in that death, you called Christ forth to new life.
You gave birth to your church,
   delivered us from the oppression of sin and death,
   and made with us a new, everlasting covenant
   by water and the Spirit.
With joy and gratitude, we break this bread
   and remember the miracles that have brought us
   to this table.
In remembrance of you and your abundant generosity,
   we will eat of this bread, even as we remember
   those who are hungry this day.
With awe and wonder, we fill this cup
   and remember the many times
   Jesus poured out his healing power.
In remembrance of you and your abundant love,
   we will drink from this cup, even as we remember
   those who thirst for love and justice.

And so, in remembrance of these,
  your miraculous acts in Christ Jesus,
  we offer ourselves in praise and thanksgiving
  as your disciples, walking with Christ,
  and proclaiming the mystery of our faith.
  Christ has died. Christ is risen.
  Christ will come again.

Communion Prayer (1 Kings 17, Galatians 1)
Pour out your Holy Spirit
  on all of us gathered here,
  that we might be your faithful disciples.
Pour out your Holy Spirit
  on these gifts of bread and wine,
    that they might be vessels of help and hope.
Walk with us in the power of your Spirit,
  that we might be one with Christ,
  one with each other,
  and one in ministry to all the world,
    until Christ comes in final victory
      and we feast at the heavenly banquet.
Through Jesus Christ,
  and with the Holy Spirit in your holy Church,
  all honor and glory is yours, Almighty God,
    now and forever more.
  Amen.

Giving the Bread and Cup
(The bread and wine are given to the people, with these or other words of blessing.)
The life of Christ revealed in you.
The love of Christ flowing through you.

SENDING FORTH

Benediction (Psalm 146, Luke 7)
Arise to life, to help, to hope!
  We arise to spread God's news.
Arise to love, to care, to give.
  We arise to be Christ for the world.

CONTEMPORARY OPTIONS

Contemporary Gathering Words (Psalm 146, Luke 7)

Listen! Our compassionate Christ, loving God,
the one who made heaven and earth,
calls to us now, here in this place,
and whispers promises of help and hope.
Listen! Our compassionate Christ, loving God,
the one who made heaven and earth,
calls to us now, here in this place,
and cries out: "Arise! Shine for the world!"

Praise Sentences (Psalm 146)

Praise the Lord, the God of heaven and earth!
Praise the Lord, O my soul!
Praise the Lord, the God of heaven and earth!
Praise the Lord, O my soul!

JUNE 13, 2010

Third Sunday after Pentecost
Joanne Carlson Brown

COLOR
Green

SCRIPTURE READINGS
1 Kings 21:1-21a; Psalm 5:1-8; Galatians 2:15-21;
Luke 7:36–8:3

THEME IDEAS
Judgment and forgiveness focus our readings. We have
people acting badly; people in distress; people who commit sins of omission; people who are deeply faithful; people who follow and support Jesus—all surrounded by the
theme of judgment and forgiveness, but a judgment and
forgiveness that belong to God, not to human beings. We
find our true selves, our true lives, in being faithful to God
and to Jesus' teachings and life. We find hope and forgiveness in a life that does not count the cost.

INVITATION AND GATHERING

Call to Worship (Psalm 5)
People of God, raise your voices in praise to God.
God takes delight in our presence here.

Come and enter God's house.
We come trusting in the steadfast love of God.
Let us worship the God of love and righteousness.

Opening Prayer (Psalm 5, 1 Kings 21, Luke 7,
Galatians 2)
O God,
    in this time of worship,
    hear our prayers.
Hear us now,
    as we stand in the midst
        of so much wrongdoing in our world.
Help us hear your voice
    amid the cacophony of sounds
        that surround and distract us.
Help us focus on what is truly important—
    living faithful lives,
    and being of service to you
        and to all your people.
May this time apart
    strengthen us to resist evil
        and to embrace justice
            in your steadfast love.
May this time with you
    focus our awareness
        that Christ lives in each one of us. Amen.

PROCLAMATION AND RESPONSE

Prayer of Confession (1 Kings 21, Galatians 2, Luke 7)
O God,
    our world seems in such a mess:
        greed triumphs over generosity;
        death appears stronger than life;
        people judge one another harshly;
        sin abounds and grace recedes far away.
Forgive us, O God,
    when we succumb to the forces
        of sin, greed, judgment, and death;

when we act as if you are not here with us;
when we fail to do the things we should:
  welcome all people with love and joy,
  live in an attitude of abundance,
  find ways to support your work in the world.
Like the woman with the alabaster jar,
  may we lay all that we are
  and all that we have at your feet,
    trusting in your forgiving, steadfast love.

Words of Assurance (Luke 7)
Sisters and brothers,
  Jesus said to the woman with the alabaster jar,
  "Your sins are forgiven."
Hear his words for yourselves,
  and take them into your heart and soul.

Passing the Peace of Christ (Galatians 2)
Sisters and brothers, look closely at the people sitting next to you. See Christ in them. Reach out your hands to greet them with signs of love and peace from the Christ that lives in you.

Response to the Word (1 Kings 21, Psalm 5, Galatians 2, Luke 7)
To words that challenge the world's values,
  to words that bring the comfort of God's presence,
  to words that speak of grace and forgiveness,
    we open our hearts.
Let these words take root in our hearts,
  that we may grow in faith.

THANKSGIVING AND COMMUNION

Invitation to Offering (Galatians 2, Luke 7)
Like the woman with the alabaster jar, let us bring all that we are, and all that we have, to support God's work in this church, this community, and this world. Offer these gifts in joy and gratitude and love, for all that God has given us—especially God's best gift of love, Jesus, who lives within us.

Offering Prayer (Psalm 5)

O God,
   through the abundance of your steadfast love,
   we are able to come into your house
      with gratitude and praise.
Accept our gifts—
   our money, our time, our very selves.
May they help forge your beloved community
   here on earth.

SENDING FORTH

Benediction (1 Kings 21, Galatians 2, Luke 7)

Go forth into the world as people reborn.
Live generosity, not greed.
Celebrate life, not death.
Revel in the abundant grace
   that flows over and through us,
   and bring that love and grace
      to a world deeply in need.
Go in peace. Amen.

CONTEMPORARY OPTIONS

Contemporary Gathering Words (Psalm 5, Luke 7)

Listen. Can you hear God's voice
   over the noise that surrounds us?
It is a voice of love, of forgiveness,
   of grace, of justice, and of peace.
Come and listen, and let your soul and body
   be refreshed and strengthened
   for the ministry to which God calls us.

Praise Sentences (Psalm 5)

In the morning God hears my voice.
In that I rejoice.
I praise God for the abundance
   of God's steadfast love.
I will worship God with all my being.

JUNE 20, 2010

Fourth Sunday after Pentecost / Father's Day

B. J. Beu

COLOR

Green

SCRIPTURE READINGS

1 Kings 19:1-15a; Psalm 42; Galatians 3:23-29; Luke 8:26-39

THEME IDEAS

Even in the midst of calamity, God is there. When Elijah was hunted and he wanted to give up, angels nurtured him and God gave him rest. The psalmist speaks of the longing of the human heart for God when events turn against us, and expresses confidence in God's help. Galatians celebrates freedom in Christ and the removal of all distinctions that society uses to judge some people of less worth than others. And Luke recalls the story of Jesus freeing the strong man from the demons and the chains that bound him. God is always there to set us free; always there to bind up our wounds; always there to lift us above the hatred we find in the world.

INVITATION AND GATHERING

Call to Worship (Psalm 42)
All who thirst, refresh yourselves in the waters
of the living God.

As a deer longs for flowing streams,
our souls long for you, O God.
All who weep, comfort yourselves in the safety
of the living God.
As a deer longs for flowing streams,
our souls long for you, O God.
All who feel lost and forgotten, find home and family
in the house of the living God.
As a deer longs for flowing streams,
our souls long for you, O God.
Come! Revive yourselves in the waters
of the living God.

Opening Prayer (1 Kings 19)
God of mystery,
  open our eyes
    to look for you in unfamiliar places;
  open our ears
    to hear you speak in the sound
      of sheer silence;
  open our hearts
    to feel the depth of your love.
When we wander in the wilderness of fear and death,
  revive us with your care,
  that we may find strength for our journey
    back to the land of hope and life. Amen.

PROCLAMATION AND RESPONSE

Prayer of Confession (Luke 8)
Liberating God,
  we come to you in our brokenness,
    yet we resist your healing touch;
  we are tormented by the demons of worry,
    of stress, of the slights of others,
      yet we fear losing our sense of self-importance
        and our righteous anger;

133

we need to be set free
from the chains that bind us,
yet we fear the true freedom you offer.
Heal us, nourish us,
and help us see ourselves and others
with compassion and love.
Help us see as Jesus sees,
and love as Jesus loves. Amen.

Assurance of Pardon (Galatians 3:25, 28-29)
Hear the words of Paul:
"Now that faith has come,
we are no longer subject to a disciplinarian,
for in Christ Jesus you are all children of God....
There is no longer Jew or Greek,
there is no longer slave or free,
there is no longer male and female;
for all of you are one in Christ Jesus.
And if you belong to Christ,
then you are Abraham's offspring,
heirs according to the promise."

Scripture Litany or Response to the Word (1 Kings 19:9b, 11-13)
Elijah, afraid and running for his life,
was confronted by the living God at Mount Horeb.
**"What are you doing here, Elijah? Go out
and stand on the mountain before the Lord,
for the Lord is about to pass by."**
Now there was a great wind—
a wind so strong that it split mountains
and broke rocks in pieces before the Lord.
But the Lord was not in the wind.
And after the wind, an earthquake shook the ground
to the roots of the mountain.
But the Lord was not in the earthquake.
And after the earthquake, a fire blazed up
toward the heavens.
But the Lord was not in the fire.

And after the fire, came a sound of sheer silence.
When Elijah heard it, he wrapped his face
in his mantle and went out and stood
at the entrance of the cave.
God speaks to us in silence.
God is speaking still.

THANKSGIVING AND COMMUNION

Offering Prayer (1 Kings 19, Luke 8)
Sovereign God,
    you feed us by your own hand,
        lest our souls shrivel
            for want of nourishment;
    you revive us with the waters of life,
        lest our hearts faint
            in the desert of our despair;
    you call us back to life and new possibilities,
        lest our hopes fail
            in our sorrow and anguish.
Accept these offerings,
    in gratitude and praise,
        for the many blessings
            we have received from your hand.
Accept the gift of our love
    and our pledge to love others
        as you have loved us. Amen.

SENDING FORTH

Benediction (1 Kings 19, Psalm 42, Galatians 3, Luke 8)
God feeds our famished souls.
We go in the nurture of Christ's love!
God fills our lives with hope for the future.
We go in the promise of Christ's love!
God frees us from the chains that bind us.
We go in the freedom of Christ's love!
God liberates us from the prisons that hold us.
We go in the new life of Christ's love!

CONTEMPORARY OPTIONS

Contemporary Gathering Words (1 Kings 19)

The wind buffets and blows,
cascading rocks down the mountainside.
Surely, God is in the wind?
The earthquake shakes and shatters,
quaking the very foundation of the earth.
Surely, God is in the earthquake?
The fire crackles and roars,
licking at the roots of life.
Surely, God is in the fire?
Where is God to be found?
Listen carefully.
God is here, in the sound of sheer silence!

Praise Sentences (Psalm 42)

Hope in God, our rock and our help.
Hope in God, our living water in the desert.
Hope in God, our song of praise.
Hope in God, our rock and our help.

JUNE 27, 2010

Fifth Sunday after Pentecost
Sara Dunning Lambert

COLOR

Green

SCRIPTURE READINGS

2 Kings 2:1-2, 6-14; Psalm 77:1-2, 11-20; Galatians 5:1, 13-25; Luke 9:51-62

THEME IDEAS

The readings from 2 Kings, Luke, and Galatians look at times of transition, turmoil, and transformation. As the time nears for Elijah to ascend to heaven within the whirlwind, Elisha discovers his unique gifts of spiritual leadership. By pledging to follow Elijah as disciple, helper, and son, he gains experience, guidance, and his teacher's blessing. Likewise, Luke speaks of the time before Christ ascends to heaven, when his disciples also learn what it will take to follow him wherever he goes. The Galatians passage adds Paul's advice to believers—to act in accord with the Holy Spirit. He urges them to become living fruit of the Spirit, using their unique gifts for the kingdom of God.

INVITATION AND GATHERING

Call to Worship (2 Kings 2, Galatians 5, Luke 9)

Throughout the ages, disciples have said,
"I will follow you wherever you go."
Lord, give us the freedom to follow you
in the ways of love.
We come from busy homes, filled with little time
to consider Christ in our lives.
Lord, give us the strength to follow you
in the ways of peace.
In times of struggle, we look to God for help.
Lord, give us the opportunity to follow you
in the ways of kindness.
Today, we celebrate the Holy Spirit,
who shows us the joy of following God.
Lord, give us the patience to follow you
in the ways of faith. Amen.

Opening Prayer (2 Kings 2, Galatians 5)

Holy One,
we come before you today:
full of hope,
full of desire,
full of promise.
Help us take up the mantle of faith
you have laid before us,
that we may use our own gifts of the Spirit
to face the challenges before us.
Help us face the turmoil
within and around us,
that we may face the future unafraid.
Show us your way, your truth,
and your life. Amen.

PROCLAMATION AND RESPONSE

Prayer of Confession (Galatians 5)

Gracious Lord,
you have blessed us with freedom—

138

freedom to follow or to turn away;
freedom to love or to hate;
freedom to heal or to hurt.
You ask only that we follow your ways,
　loving our neighbors as ourselves.
In the midst of our turbulent lives,
　help us find teachers
　　to show us the gifts you set within us.
And help us claim these gifts today.

Words of Assurance (Galatians 5)
Harvest the fruit of the Spirit, freely given by God,
　and share it freely with others.
Know that you are loved and forgiven.
Trust that you are treasured, now and always. Amen.

Passing the Peace of Christ (2 Kings 2, Luke 9)
Disciples have said to their teachers, "I will follow you
wherever you go." May the peace of Christ follow you
wherever you go: at home, at work, and in the world. Let us
turn to one another and offer signs of this peace in our lives.

Response to the Word (2 Kings 2, Galatians 5)
We have each been fashioned for a unique purpose; each
been given unique gifts; each been blessed with varying
abilities. During times of turmoil and transition, we can
choose to become stagnant, or we can choose to be transformed by God's love. When we choose transformation,
we choose to fully share in the vision of a community led
by the Spirit—a community of love, gentleness, self-
control, joy, patience, peace, faithfulness, kindness, and
generosity. When we follow Christ, we take up his mantle,
moving forward together. May we all say, "I will follow
you wherever you go."

THANKSGIVING AND COMMUNION

Offering Prayer (Galatians 5)
Receive our humble offerings, O Lord,
　for your work in the world.

Bless those who give,
  those who send,
  and those who will receive these gifts.
May our offering sow seeds of hope
  and bear the fruit of love
    wherever they are sown.

Invitation to Communion or Communion Prayer
As the prophets of old knew, so may we also know. When we live by the Spirit, we will inherit the kingdom of God. The Spirit of love and forgiveness grows on the tree of life. This Spirit is available to all who seek it. Eat of this fruit, for it is the body of Christ, given for you.

SENDING FORTH

Benediction (Galatians 5, Luke 9)
May the transforming love of God
  work in your lives, today and always.
Go forth into the world with peace, love, and joy.
Follow Christ wherever he leads you.
Fulfill the promise found in the fruit of the Spirit. Amen.

CONTEMPORARY OPTIONS

Contemporary Gathering Words (2 Kings 2, Luke 9)
We gather today as a community led by the Spirit.
  Your way, O God, is holy.
Pick up the mantle of faith and follow Christ today.
  Your way, O God, is holy.
Listen, pray, and believe.
  Your way, O God, is holy.

Praise Sentences (Galatians 5, Luke 9)
The fruit of the Spirit is love, joy, peace, patience,
  kindness, generosity, faithfulness, gentleness,
  and self-control.
Christ has set us free!
Follow Christ and know God's love!

JULY 4, 2010

Sixth Sunday after Pentecost

Hans Holznagel

COLOR
Green

SCRIPTURE READINGS
2 Kings 5:1-14; Psalm 30; Galatians 6:(1-6) 7-16; Luke 10:1-11, 16-20

THEME IDEAS
Gentleness and a firm stance for peace are paths to healing, right relationships, and God's realm—even for the mighty, the prosperous, and the strong. Naaman almost allows his ego to prevent his own healing. Jesus sends out seventy ambassadors, brandishing nothing more than words of peace, acts of healing, and belief in God's realm. Paul urges gentleness with "transgressors." On this birthday of our country, what lessons can we draw? What stance might we take? What healing might turn the world's mourning into dancing?

INVITATION AND GATHERING

Call to Worship (Psalm 30)
Sing praises to God, O faithful ones.
    Give thanks and proclaim God's holy name.
Weeping or joyful, mourning or dancing,
    come as you are, for all are welcome here.

Open your hearts to healing, to life restored.
Let us worship God.

Opening Prayer (2 Kings 5, Galatians 6, Luke 10)
O God of cleansing waters,
    center our hearts on healing.
Messenger of peace,
    instruct us in your ways.
Spirit of gentleness,
    make of us a new creation.
Amen.

PROCLAMATION AND RESPONSE

Prayer of Confession (2 Kings 5, Psalm 30)
O God of people and nations,
    we are ignorant and arrogant
        about our own prosperity and might.
When we forget how much we have,
    remind us of our abundance.
When we take pride in our status
    and think ourselves better than others,
        grant us humility.
When we use wealth and power
    to get our own way at the expense of others,
        correct us.
Heal us, we pray,
    that we may be a force for wholeness.
With all that we have,
    we pray for your forgiveness. Amen.

Words of Assurance (Psalm 30)
God's anger lasts but a moment,
    but God's favor lasts a lifetime.
Weeping may last the night,
    but joy comes in the morning.
God takes off our sackcloth
    and clothes us with joy.
Let us rejoice! We are forgiven!

Passing the Peace of Christ (Luke 10)
Jesus sent forth his disciples with a word of peace. We too are bearers of that peace as we greet others in Christ's name. Please greet your neighbors with the blessing: "The peace of Christ be with you."

Response to the Word (Luke 10)
Equip us to know your will, O God,
   as we strive to labor daily
   in the fields of your harvest. Amen

THANKSGIVING AND COMMUNION

Invitation to the Offering (Galatians 6)
"You reap whatever you sow," says the Apostle Paul, "so wherever we have the opportunity, let us work for the good of all." For the nurture of this family of faith, and for the ministry to a world in need, let us now give joyfully as we present our tithes and offerings.

Offering Prayer (Galatians 6)
Generous God, source of all abundance,
   bless now these gifts, we pray.
Receive this offering.
Receive our very lives.
Fit us for humble, joyful ministry
   in your name. Amen.

SENDING FORTH

Benediction (Galatians 6)
Do not grow weary in doing what is right,
   for you will reap a great harvest
     if you do not give up.
Sow in the Spirit
   and reap the blessings of God.
Go in peace.

CONTEMPORARY OPTIONS

Contemporary Gathering Words (Psalm 30)

You cried all night,
   your life is the pits,
   you're very sorry for something you've done;
      but dawn has broken
      and joy comes in the morning.
If you can't feel the dawn, take heart. It's coming.
If joy still feels a long way off, you're not alone.
Let's be in Christ's healing presence this hour.
Let's give our thanks and praise to God.

Praise Sentences (Psalm 30, Luke 10)

Make our spirits dance, O God!
   Take off our sackcloth and clothe us with joy!
Help our souls praise you and not be silent!
   Take off our sackcloth and clothe us with joy!
Teach the way of peace, O Jesus!
   Take off our sackcloth and clothe us with joy!

JULY 11, 2010

Seventh Sunday after Pentecost
Mary J. Scifres

COLOR
Green

SCRIPTURE READINGS
Amos 7:7-17; Psalm 82; Colossians 1:1-14; Luke 10:25-37

THEME IDEAS
Knowledge of God leads to love—perfect love, complete love—love of God, of neighbor, even of self. In the letter to the Colossians and in Luke's Gospel, wisdom emerges as a path to love. Amos and the psalmist remind the Hebrew people that God's law is only fulfilled when the people pursue justice and righteousness. To truly comprehend God's grace is to fulfill God's law by loving even the least among us.

INVITATION AND GATHERING

Call to Worship (Luke 10)
Love the Lord your God.
We come with love and hope!
Love your neighbors too.
We come with loving hearts.
Love even yourself.
We come in humble trust.

Love and you will live.
**We come to worship, that God's love
might live in us.**

Opening Prayer (Luke 10)

God of Samaritans and Palestinians,
    God of Arabs and Americans,
    God of friends and foes,
    God of all who call the earth their home—
        walk with us in this time of worship;
        walk with us on this journey of life.
Help us see the humanity of the foreigner
    lying injured by the side of the road.
Help us respond to the needs all around us.
Help us overcome our fear of strangers,
    our hatred of enemies.
Encourage us,
    that we may be servants to all,
        be they family or foe,
        stranger or friend,
        Arab or American.
In the name of Christ
    who walks with us, we pray. Amen.

PROCLAMATION AND RESPONSE

Prayer of Confession (Luke 10)

God of judgment and grace,
    we pour out our hearts to you now.
Hear our prayers
    as we remember the times
        we have seen others in need,
            yet turned away.
(Moment of silence)
Hear our prayers
    as we remember the times
        we have judged a stranger
        or hated an enemy.

(Moment of silence)
Hear our prayers
  as we remember the times
    we have withheld our love and care.
(Moment of silence)
Forgive us, gracious God,
  when we have missed opportunities
    to live as you would have us live.
In Jesus' name,
  we remember and we pray. Amen.

Words of Assurance (Colossians 1, Luke 10)
The one who calls us to show mercy
  has shown us mercy.
God knows of your faith
  and the love that you have in your hearts.
In the name of our merciful God, you are forgiven!

Passing the Peace of Christ (Luke 10)
Those who show mercy embody Christ to the world. Let
us share signs of mercy and peace with one another.

Response to the Word (Luke 10)
What must we do to inherit abundant life?
  Love the Lord your God.
How much must we love?
  With all our heart and soul, strength and mind.
Whom else must we love?
  Our neighbors, near and far.
Even neighbors we know and neighbors we fear?
  Friends and enemies, strangers and family.
How can we love all those?
  Because Christ first loved us.
Must we love ourselves too?
  We must first love ourselves
    if we wish to love at all.

THANKSGIVING AND COMMUNION

Invitation to the Offering (Luke 10)
The good Samaritan bandaged the wounds of a neighbor
in need, gave him shelter, and paid for his care. May we
open our hearts, our lives, and even our wallets with
Samaritan-like generosity.

Offering Prayer (Luke 10)
Generous, loving God,
    bless the gifts we have given.
As we give of ourselves,
    bless our hearts,
        that we may love more fully.
Through our gifts,
    may the weak and needy find healing and comfort
        for the wounds of their lives. Amen.

SENDING FORTH

Benediction (Colossians 1, Luke 10)
May you be made strong with the strength
of God's glorious power.
    May we be humble with the gentleness of grace.
May you endure with patience the struggles of life.
    May we slow down to notice the struggles
    of others.
May you joyfully give thanks to Christ
who has shown us the way.
    May we live our gratitude by helping others
    as God has helped us. Amen.

CONTEMPORARY OPTIONS

Contemporary Gathering Words (Luke 10)
It is a familiar story:
    a lawyer comes to test Jesus,
    and Jesus responds with a question.

It is a familiar story:
  the lawyer has all the right answers,
  even to the very end.
It is a familiar story:
  the religious people and the priest
  pass by their brother in need.
It is a familiar story:
  the Palestinian terrorist stops to give aid.
Wait a second! That's not what Luke says!
Perhaps the familiar story is not so familiar.
A Samaritan was hated and feared,
  considered sinful and dangerous.
This is our story:
  we test God, and God responds
  with more questions than answers.
This is our story:
  even those with all the right answers
  must eventually live the answers.
This is our story:
  when we are perfectly busy and perfectly happy,
  we may miss the most important message of all.
Love. Love. Love.
It is a familiar story:
  a story much easier to remember than to live,
  a message much easier to say than to do.

Praise Sentences (Colossians 1, Luke 10)

Love God with all your heart.
  Give thanks and praise God's name!
Love God with all your soul.
  Give thanks and praise God's name!
Love God with all your strength.
  Give thanks and praise God's name!
Love God with all your mind.
  Give thanks and praise God's name!

JULY 18, 2010

Eighth Sunday after Pentecost
Rebecca J. Kruger Gaudino

COLOR

Green

SCRIPTURE READINGS

Amos 8:1-12; Psalm 52; Colossians 1:15-28; Luke 10:38-42

THEME IDEAS

The theme of hospitality binds all our readings together. Speaking to the social elite, who believe their own lives and welfare are the sole focus of life, Amos describes a community where the wealthy and powerful make life unlivable for the powerless. Amos warns of a time when the Guest will also find life in their midst unlivable. The writer of Colossians describes Jesus Christ as the "first-born" of all creation—the one who establishes in the faith and his body those who are estranged from God. Luke tells the story of Martha, who welcomes Jesus into her home, but then does not find time to join the Guest, as does Mary. How do we welcome and make space for God and for others in the ways we order our own lives and the life of our communities?

INVITATION AND GATHERING

Call to Worship (Psalm 52)

Seek refuge in God!
Like green olive trees in the house of God,
we dwell in the steadfast love of God
forever and ever.
Seek refuge in God!
We put our trust in God,
because of God's mighty deeds.
Seek refuge in God!
In the presence of the faithful,
we proclaim God's holy name.

Opening Prayer (Psalm 52, Colossians 1)

We come to your house
seeking your presence, O God.
For in the mystery of our universe,
you created all things in heaven and on earth
and reconciled all things to you,
by and in Jesus Christ.
So we stand before you
steadfast in the hope
promised by our brother, Jesus. Amen.

PROCLAMATION AND RESPONSE

Prayer of Confession (Psalm 52, Amos 8, Luke 10)

O God,
we lead busy lives.
Just coming to church on Sunday mornings
often seems like a sacrifice.
There's so much to do,
so much to worry about.
We read about being an olive tree
planted in your house, green and flourishing,
under the care of your presence.

Yet, our roots feel planted most anywhere else:
in our duties; in our business relationships;
in our family plans; in our volunteer commitments;
in our efforts to make it in this world.
When we forget who we are,
when the soil of our lives becomes barren,
plant our roots in your goodness and wisdom,
that we may welcome you into our lives.
Amen.

Words of Assurance (Psalm 52, Colossians 1)
Trust in the steadfast love of God forever and ever.
Claim the hope promised by the good news:
God welcomes all to this house,
even those who have been estranged from God!

Passing the Peace of Christ (Colossians 1)
The fullness of God dwelled in Jesus Christ our brother,
who showed us the ways of love and peace. As the body
of Christ in the world, let us share his love and peace with
one another.

Response to the Word (Luke 10)
Holy God,
you care for our needs
with your compassionate presence
and teachings.
Holy God,
be our Guest,
accept our seeking presence,
and bless us with understanding. Amen.

THANKSGIVING AND COMMUNION

Invitation to the Offering (Amos 8, Colossians 1)
As Amos observed long ago, in our world the poor are too
often sold for silver and the needy for a pair of sandals.
But we can live a different ethic—our lives can embody
the love of God. Let's make room for others through our
giving, that they may also know God's love and hope.

Offering Prayer (Amos 8, Psalm 52)
The vast inequities of our world
grieve you, O God.
Use our gifts
to lift up those who suffer injustice
and who need your hope and presence. Amen.

SENDING FORTH

Benediction (Psalm 52)
We leave the house of God,
but not the presence of God.
Let us root ourselves deeply in God's holy presence
and live out God's love for all.
Trust in the steadfast love of God forever and ever.

CONTEMPORARY OPTIONS

Contemporary Gathering Words (Psalm 52)
Be like olive trees in the house of God—
green and flourishing, full and verdant.
We will grow strong in the house of God—
deeply rooted, well watered.
Be like olive trees in the house of God—
seeking God's refuge, trusting God's care.
We will dwell in the house of God,
and proclaim God's name forever!

Praise Sentences (Colossians 1)
Jesus Christ is the image of the invisible God,
the firstborn of all creation!
In Christ, all things hold together!
Trust in Christ's love forever!
In Christ, all things are blessed!
Trust in Christ's love forever!
Thanks be to God!

JULY 25, 2010

Ninth Sunday after Pentecost
John A. Brewer

COLOR
Green

SCRIPTURE READINGS
Hosea 1:2-10; Psalm 85; Colossians 2:6-15 (16-19);
Luke 11:1-13

THEME IDEAS
As people anticipate the "lazy days of summer," these
texts are helpful reminders of persistence and reliance,
and of Christian discipleship. The psalmist proclaims the
"unfailing" love and mercy of God. Hosea highlights the
consequences of humanity's attempt at self-reliance. Luke
teaches that, through prayer, we can rely upon God to
meet our needs. Paul reminds us that we are dependent
upon the very person of Jesus Christ—for we are rooted,
built up, and strengthened in him alone.

INVITATION AND GATHERING

Call to Worship (Psalm 85)
Come! Join the fellowship of God's people—
people who gather as faithful disciples of Christ.
We seek the One who frees us
from uncertainty and doubt.

Come! Join the welcome of God's people—
people who meet together for justice and peace.
We seek the One who is trustworthy,
the One who gives us what is good.
Come! Join the celebration of God's people—
people of the One who was, and is, and shall ever be.
We raise our voices in praise and honor to God,
and worship the One who is faithful.

Opening Prayer (Colossians 2)

God of grace and God of glory,
   come and be known to us
      in our gathering together;
   come and be present in the songs we sing
      and in the prayers we raise.
From the busy byways of life,
   we come to find once again
      that you are always present
         and always ready to receive us.
As we affirm our faith this day,
   deepen the roots of our commitment,
      that we may learn your calling upon our lives.
Surround us now
   with the love and comfort of your Holy Spirit
      and the direction and redemption of Christ. Amen.

PROCLAMATION AND RESPONSE

Prayer of Confession (Hosea 1)

O Lord of mercy and compassion,
   we bare our souls before you
      in this hour of worship and prayer.
We have been unfaithful to you
   and have forsaken the Covenant Love
      you have shared with us.
For our wandering, wayward ways,
   hear our confessions of sin and selfishness
      and offer us your forgiveness.

We ask for forgiveness
  and the strength to behave as your true children,
    as your very people, the Church.
It is the redeeming Christ
  before whom we bow
  and before whom we confess our need.
We come to you in hope of redemption. Amen.

Words of Assurance (Luke 11)

Seek and you will find.
Knock and the door will be opened to you.
Ask and it will be given to you.
God has promised us grace and forgiveness
  in the love of Jesus Christ.
Come home again and be the people God intended.

Response to the Word (Luke 11)

Like a true friend, Lord,
  you have not withheld
    the wisdom of your word.
Like a true friend, Lord,
  you have given us the nourishment and strength
    for the living of these days.

THANKSGIVING AND COMMUNION

Invitation to the Offering (Colossians 2)

Having received the grace of God in the redemption of
Christ, we live strengthened in the faith, with hearts overflowing with thankfulness. From the depths of our hearts,
we offer to God the very best we have. May our offering
be a true act of worship and thanksgiving.

Offering Prayer

Before you, O God,
  we offer our prayers, our presence, our gifts,
    and our service.

We lay our gifts before you
in praise and thanksgiving
for your many blessings.
May these offerings
continue the transforming work of your Spirit
in and through our congregation. Amen.

Invitation to Communion (Luke 11)
Come and receive the answer to your prayers. This cup
and this loaf contain the fulfillment of the human heart.
Through this sacrament, we receive the power and direction to bring about the kingdom of God—as God's will is
done on earth as it is in heaven. Come and receive the answer to your prayers.

SENDING FORTH

Benediction (Psalm 85)
As you go forth,
know that you leave
with the unfailing love of God.
As you leave this place,
know that by God's strength
you will be able to face the challenges
of the coming week.
As you return to your daily lives,
know that your pursuit of peace
reveals to the world
that you are God's children. Amen.

CONTEMPORARY OPTIONS

Contemporary Gathering Words (Hosea 1)
God has been looking for you.
Where have you been off to this time?
We have been around.
There are so many distractions in our lives.
How long has it been?
It's been too long since we were reminded
of God's unrelenting love.

Are you ready?
**We're ready. We're exhausted chasing
the elusive dreams of the world. We need God!**
Then come home. Come back to the place
where you are loved, no matter what.
**Gladly we come home. Gladly we are here.
Gladly we sing of the welcoming love of God!**

Praise Sentences (Colossians 2)

Praise God for being everything we need,
for filling the emptiness of our lives!
Praise God for giving us ultimate victory
over sin and death!
Let there be glory and honor and praises
to Jesus Christ, who is our new beginning!

AUGUST 1, 2010

Tenth Sunday after Pentecost
Mary J. Scifres

COLOR
Green

SCRIPTURE READINGS
Hosea 11:1-11; Psalm 107:1-9, 43; Colossians 3:1-11; Luke 12:13-21

THEME IDEAS
Although these divergent scriptures do not have a common focus, compassionate, generous living is reflected in each. In Hosea, God proclaims how set apart the Holy One truly is—choosing compassion instead of judgment for the Israelites who have turned away. In Luke, the rich man in Jesus' parable proves his humanness by choosing worldly wealth over heavenly values. Jesus, like the writer of Colossians, invites us to choose God's holy path. We are all invited to roar with generosity, to tremble with compassion, and to clothe ourselves in mercy and love. We are invited to be made new, to be made Christlike and godly for the sake of the kingdom.

INVITATION AND GATHERING

Call to Worship (Psalm 107, Colossians 3, Luke 12, Matthew 6)
Come into God's presence with thanksgiving and praise.
Seeking God, we come to find new life and joy.

Come into God's presence with hunger and thirst.
Seeking God, we hunger for mercy and love.
Come into God's presence with confidence and hope.
For in seeking, we will find.
In hungering, we will be fed.
In loving, we will be loved.
In treasuring, we will be treasured.
Come into God's presence, for you are God's
greatest delight!

Opening Prayer (Psalm 107, Colossians 3, Luke 12)
Steadfast and loving God,
    we turn our hearts and minds to you.
Put to death those thoughts
    that would separate us
        from your loving presence in our lives.
Clothe us in compassion and mercy.
Bind us together,
    that we may be one people, the body of Christ,
        your children of love in this world. Amen.

PROCLAMATION AND RESPONSE

Prayer of Confession (Hosea 11, Colossians 3, Luke 12)
Merciful God,
    warm us with your compassion.
Forgive us,
    when we turn away from your love.
Gather us closer,
    when we pull away from you.
Clothe us with your grace,
    when we surround ourselves
        with worldly desires and passions.
Renew our zeal to follow you
    when you see us pursue values
        that destroy our lives
            and the lives of others around us.

Roar with mighty love, dear God,
that we might hear your voice
and heed your call.
In Christ's name, we pray. Amen.

Words of Assurance (Hosea 11, Psalm 107, Colossians 3)
Hear the words of the Most High:
"How can I give you up?
How can I hand you over?
My compassion grows warm and tender.
I will not execute my anger or destroy my beloved.
I am the God of steadfast love
and I will clothe you in compassion and mercy.
In the name of Christ, you are my beloved
and forgiven children!"

Passing the Peace of Christ (Hosea 11, Colossians 3)
Clothed in God's mercy, let us share together signs of unity and peace.

Response to the Word (Colossians 3)
Seek first the things of God.
We are created in God's own image.
Set your minds on things above.
We are children of eternal life.
Clothe yourselves in this newness of life.
In Christ we have been born anew!

THANKSGIVING AND COMMUNION

Invitation to the Offering (Luke 12)
Christ warns us: "Be on guard against all kinds of greed; for one's life does not consist in the abundance of possessions." Therefore, let us store up for ourselves treasures in heaven as we share our earthly treasures with a world in need.

Offering Prayer (Psalm 107)

Thank you for your steadfast love
  and generous compassion.
Thank you for the gifts of this earth.
As we share our gifts with your church,
  help us know the fulfillment
    of generous living.
Use these gifts to satisfy our thirst for justice
  and to fill our world with goodness.

Invitation to Communion (Psalm 107, Colossians 3)

Come, all who are thirsty for compassion,
  for in Christ your thirst will be quenched.
Come, all who hunger for justice and hope,
  for in Christ, you will be fed.
Come, all who yearn for love and community,
  for in the body of Christ, you are loved!

SENDING FORTH

Benediction (Luke 12)

My friends, go into the world
  with compassion and love.
Store up treasures in heaven,
  even as the earth and its people
    receive the treasure that is you!

CONTEMPORARY OPTIONS

Contemporary Gathering Words (Colossians 3, Matthew 6)

We, who have been raised with Christ,
are invited to set our minds on things above.
  We seek first the kingdom of God.
We, whose lives are hidden in Christ,
are called to clothe ourselves with new life.
  We ask and it is given to us.

We, whose lives are reflections of God,
are called to live with mercy and compassion.
**We knock and the door of God's love
is opened to shine through our lives.**

Praise Sentences (Psalm 107)
Give thanks to the Lord, our God of love,
whose love endures forever.
Give thanks to the Lord!

AUGUST 8, 2010

Eleventh Sunday after Pentecost
Mary J. Scifres

COLOR
Green

SCRIPTURE READINGS
Isaiah 1:1, 10-20; Psalm 50:1-8, 22-23; Hebrews 11:1-3, 8-16; Luke 12:32-40

THEME IDEAS
Like last week's readings, each of today's scriptures easily stands alone, but the true treasures of God's kingdom shine through each reading. God prophesies through Isaiah that we must cleanse ourselves of evil and focus on goodness and justice. In Hebrews, we are reminded to be people of faith and hope. In Luke, Jesus calls us to set our priorities in line with God's priorities, to be ready for the in-breaking of God's realm, here and now. Get ready! This is a day not only to get our priorities in order, but to act on those priorities with purpose and passion.

INVITATION AND GATHERING

Call to Worship (Psalm 50, Luke 12)
God calls to us, "Gather, my faithful ones!"
We gather with faith and hope.
God calls to us, "Honor me with gratitude and praise."
We sing with thanks and joy.

God calls to us, "Be ready for anything!"
**We worship with candles brightly burning
and hearts prepared for God's presence.
Come, Lord Jesus, come!**

Opening Prayer (Isaiah 1, Luke 12)
Mighty God,
you are always dressed for action.
Quick to forgive and ready to respond,
you grace us with your care and compassion
in so many ways.
Strengthen us to be a people
dressed for action and ready to respond.
As we light candles for worship,
light your passion within us,
that we may be always aware
of your world and its needs;
of your presence in our lives;
of your calling in this world.
Cleanse us with your love,
that we might hear your word
and respond to your call. Amen.

PROCLAMATION AND RESPONSE

Prayer of Confession (Isaiah 1, Psalm 50, Luke 12)
Wash us clean, dear God.
Cleanse us of all evil.
Forgive us when we treasure things that don't matter.
Forgive us when our choices bring harm to others.
Gather us into the light of your presence.
Wash over us with your mercy and forgiveness.
In Christ's name, we pray. Amen.

Words of Assurance (Isaiah 1)
Though our sins may be like scarlet,
Christ has made them whiter than snow.
God will remove the evil of our actions,
even as we learn to do good and seek justice.

In Christ, we are forgiven!
In Christ, we are restored to be the children of God!
Amen and amen!

Passing the Peace of Christ (Hebrews 11, Luke 12)
Now faith is the assurance of things hoped for, the conviction of things not seen. But here and now, we can see God's love shining through our neighbors. Come, let us share together the light of God's love as we greet one another with the peace of Christ.

Response to the Word (Luke 12)
You must be ready, for God comes
at unexpected times in unexpected places.
Expect the unexpected!
Dress for action, for God requires
our hands and feet, here and now.
Put on the clothing of compassion!
Light your lamps, for the world needs to see
God's light and love.
We are the light of the world!

THANKSGIVING AND COMMUNION

Invitation to the Offering (Luke 12)
Do not be afraid, my friends, to share of yourselves and your gifts. It is God's good pleasure to give you the kingdom. Sell your possessions. Give your gifts. For we are promised unfailing treasure in heaven!

Offering Prayer (Luke 12)
We thank you for the many gifts
of our lives and our world.
May these gifts we return to you
shine like a beacon of love and compassion
to a world in need.
Bless us to be a people of faith and faithful giving,
that we are always ready to see and to serve
where needed. Amen.

SENDING FORTH

Benediction (Luke 12)
Go forth dressed for action!
We are ready to love and to serve!
Light your lamps for all to see!
We will shine with the light of God's love!

CONTEMPORARY OPTIONS

Contemporary Gathering Words (Isaiah 1)
Wash yourselves in God's love.
Bathe in the light of Christ.
Listen for the wind of the Spirit.
God is with us here.
God is with us now.
(A time of silence for reflection may follow.)

Praise Sentences (Psalm 50)
Praise and thanksgiving to God!
Praise and thanksgiving to God!

AUGUST 15, 2010

Twelfth Sunday after Pentecost

B. J. Beu

COLOR

Green

SCRIPTURE READINGS

Isaiah 5:1-7; Psalm 80:1-2, 8-19; Hebrews 11:29–12:2;
Luke 12:49-56

THEME IDEAS

Isaiah and the psalmist proclaim that God lovingly
planted the vineyard Israel. Both agree that the vineyard's
walls have fallen and the vineyard is being destroyed. But
whereas Isaiah claims that this is God's doing as a conse-
quence of Israel's sin, the psalmist holds out hope that
God will yet save the people and give them new life. Hebrews implores us to follow the great cloud of witnesses
who have set aside the weight of sin and death that we
may look to Christ, the perfecter of our faith. In Luke,
Jesus yearns to bring fire to the earth to bring true judgment to us all. God is not just the one who plants us like
a vineyard, God is the one who destroys the vineyard that
bears bad fruit. And yet we look to this same God, in the
midst of our destruction, for our salvation—salvation
through fire and baptism. The great cloud of witnesses
testifies to our need to follow Christ, who is our hope.

INVITATION AND GATHERING

Call to Worship *(Isaiah 5, Psalm 80, Hebrews 11)*

We are the fruit of God's vineyard,
protected by the walls of God's love.
**May we be plantings of justice
and righteousness, not of bloodshed
and violence against the poor.**
We are the fruit of God's vineyard,
watered by the rains of God's Spirit.
**May we grow healthy and strong,
bearing the fruit of salvation.**
We are the fruit of God's vineyard,
rooted in Christ, the perfecter of our faith.
**May we flourish in the soil of God's joy,
joining the great cloud of witnesses before us.**

Opening Prayer *(Isaiah 5, Psalm 80)*

God of the vineyard,
plant your passion
for justice and righteousness
in the soil of our lives;
prune our thirst
for bloodshed and strife
in the wells of our self-interest
and greed;
make room in our hearts
for compassion and generosity.
Nurture us in this time of worship,
that we may bear good fruit
and live as your people—
a people of passion
for justice and righteousness.

PROCLAMATION AND RESPONSE

Prayer of Confession *(Isaiah 5, Luke 12)*

Bountiful God,
secure in your loving care,

we have grown complacent:
   neglecting the poor among us,
   forsaking the paths of righteousness,
   ignoring the weighty matters of the law.
Dress us with your forgiveness.
Prune away our selfishness.
Draw down the fire of your baptism
   that we may be reborn
      in the ashes of your refiner's fire. Amen.

Words of Assurance (Hebrews 12)
Looking to Christ, the pioneer of our faith,
   we find our sins forgiven.
Loving others through Christ's perfect love for us,
   we are made whole and one with God.

Response to the Word (Isaiah 5, Psalm 80, Hebrews 12)
O Christ, perfecter of our faith,
   may the words we have heard
      bear fruit in our lives.
Teach us the path of the cross—
   that we might be strengthened
      for the race of faith;
   that we might run it
      with diligence and courage. Amen.

THANKSGIVING AND COMMUNION

Offering Prayer (Isaiah 5, Psalm 80)
Faithful God,
   your love for us is like sunlight
      that blesses young vines in a vineyard;
   your passion for our salvation is like rain
      that kisses the ground to bring forth life.
With joy for your bounty,
   we bring our gifts before you this day,
   that your vineyard may increase
      through the care of our labor
         and the treasure of our purse. Amen.

SENDING FORTH

Benediction (Isaiah 5, Luke 12)
We are the fruit of God's vineyard.
Go and bear the fruit of justice and righteousness.
We go to build the kingdom of God!
We are the fruit of God's vineyard.
Go and bear the fruit of mercy and peace.
We go to build the kingdom of God!
We are the fruit of God's vineyard.
Go and bear the fruit of love to the stranger
and hope to the despairing.
We go to build the kingdom of God!
Go with the courage of Christ!

CONTEMPORARY OPTIONS

Contemporary Gathering Words (Hebrews 12, Luke 12)
This is the place where saints worship.
This is the place where sinners are baptized
with fire and the Spirit.
This is the place where faith abounds.
This is the place where doubts are welcome.
This is the place where Christ perfects us.
This is a place where Christ redeems us
with love and grace.
Let us acquire the fire and rekindle our faith!

Praise Sentences (Isaiah 5, Psalm 80)
Sing praise of God's vineyard!
Sing praise of Christ's light!
Sing praise of God's salvation!
Sing praise of Christ's light!

AUGUST 22, 2010

Thirteenth Sunday after Pentecost
B. J. Beu

COLOR
Green

SCRIPTURE READINGS
Jeremiah 1:4-10; Psalm 71:1-6; Hebrews 12:18-29;
Luke 13:10-17

THEME IDEAS
Rescue is a theme that runs throughout today's scriptures.
Before Jeremiah was born, God had consecrated him to be
a prophet—to rescue God's people from aimlessness and
sin. The psalmist seeks refuge in the God who rescues us
from earthly perils. Hebrews takes this idea to a cosmic
level, indicating that the whole created order will be shaken,
and that Christ has come as a mediator to rescue us from all
that does not endure. In Luke, Jesus rescues a woman from
an infirmity she has suffered with for eighteen years. In a
world full of peril, rebellion, and decay, God is present to
rescue us and offer us a kingdom that cannot be shaken.

INVITATION AND GATHERING

Call to Worship (Jeremiah 1, Psalm 71, Luke 13)
O God, you are our rock and our refuge.
You are our fortress in times of trouble.
   Come, O God, and protect us!

O Lord, you save us from the hand of the wicked.
You deliver us from our foes.
Come, O Lord, and save us!
O Christ, you heal us from our infirmities.
You release us from the chains that bind us.
Come, O blessed one, and make us whole!

Opening Prayer (Luke 13)

Great Healer,
  like the woman in the synagogue,
  we come before you
    bent and beaten down
      by the suffering in our lives.
Free us from the demons
  that shackle our spirit.
Make us whole, O God,
  that we may be a people of healing.
Set us free from all that binds us,
  that we may break the chains of others.
Amen.

PROCLAMATION AND RESPONSE

Prayer of Confession (Jeremiah 1)

Eternal God,
  before we were conceived
    in our mothers' womb,
    you called us as your own.
When we stray from the path you set before us,
  return us to your ways.
When we doubt the gifts you have given us,
  restore our confidence.
When we look to our own wisdom,
  refocus our attention on your teachings.
When we question whether you are with us,
  grant us the confidence to go forth unafraid,
  that the world may be blessed
    through the example of our lives. Amen.

Assurance of Pardon (Jeremiah 1)

Just as God touched Jeremiah's mouth,
    giving him words to speak,
God touches our lives,
    making us whole.
God accepts each of us as beloved children,
    giving us strength for the journey.

Response to the Word (Jeremiah 1, Psalm 71)

Listen, God has called us.
We will heed the words of the Lord.
Listen, God has a word for us to share with the world.
We will heed the words of the Lord.
Listen, God has called us to be Christ's disciples.
We will heed the words of the Lord.

THANKSGIVING AND COMMUNION

Offering Prayer (Psalm 71, Hebrews 12)

God of power and might,
    in times of trial,
        you are our one true refuge,
        our fortress against the storm;
    in times of uncertainty and doubt,
        you rescue us from gloom and despair.
In thanksgiving and praise,
    we offer you our tithes and offerings,
    we offer you our very lives,
        that we might know
            your unshakable kingdom. Amen.

SENDING FORTH

Benediction (Jeremiah 1, Luke 13)

God has set us free.
God releases us from bondage.
Christ has made us whole.
Christ heals our every wound.

The Spirit has strengthened us for the journey.
God's Spirit sends us forth.
Go with the confidence of God's anointed.

CONTEMPORARY OPTIONS

Contemporary Call to Worship (Hebrews 12)
God is shaking the earth.
Is there anywhere to stand?
We stand on the promises of God.
God is shaking the earth.
Is there anywhere to find support?
We lean on the everlasting arms of God.
God is shaking the earth.
Is there anywhere to look for our salvation?
We look to Jesus, the mediator
of a new covenant—a covenant of life
in the midst of death.

Praise Sentences (Luke 13)
God has set us free.
Praise God!
Christ has made us whole.
Praise Christ!
The Spirit has brought us peace.
Praise the Spirit!

AUGUST 29, 2010

Fourteenth Sunday after Pentecost
Mary J. Scifres

COLOR
Green

SCRIPTURE READINGS
Jeremiah 2:4-13; Psalm 81:1, 10-16; Hebrews 13:1-8, 15-16; Luke 14:1, 7-14

THEME IDEAS
Today's readings bring into sharp focus a danger of contemporary life: when we follow our self-interested pursuits, we lose sight of God's priorities of justice and mercy. Through Jeremiah, God laments the worthless pursuits of the Israelites, and in Psalm 81, God yearns for their return. In both Hebrews and Luke we are advised to focus on the values of servanthood, sharing, and loving. We live in a world where such values are dethroned while financial, material, and personal success are placed on pedestals to guide our lives. Today's scriptures illustrate the emptiness of such pursuits, offering instead the finest wheat of God's love and guidance in our lives.

INVITATION AND GATHERING

Call to Worship (Psalm 81)
God is our strength!
Sing it loud.

Christ is our joy!
Shout it for all to hear.
Sing of love and grace!
Shout of mercy and truth!
Sing of God's goodness!
Shout of Christ's love!

Opening Prayer (Jeremiah 2, Hebrews 13, Luke 14)

God of days ancient and new,
    speak to us your ancient words of wisdom.
Help us hear afresh
    Christ's message of love and servanthood.
Soften our hearts
    to sense your presence.
Open our eyes
    to see your guiding hand.
Open our ears
    to hear your call.
Change our lives
    to follow your path
        of justice and mercy.
In Christ's name, we pray. Amen.

PROCLAMATION AND RESPONSE

Prayer of Confession (Psalm 81, Hebrews 13, Luke 14)

Servant God,
    we often lose our way.
Forgive us,
    when we focus exclusively
        on the values of strength and might;
    when we accept the world's measures
        of power and success;
    when we scramble for social recognition
        and the seat of honor at the table of life;
    when we withhold hospitality to strangers
        or forget the tortured and tormented
            of our world;

when we betray our marital vows
 or neglect our loved ones.
Turn our hearts back to you,
 that we might again be your people.
Open our ears and minds,
 that we might hear your voice
 and answer your call.
In hope and trust, we pray. Amen.

Words of Assurance (Psalm 81)
When we open our hearts,
 God promises to fill our hungry souls.
When we listen and walk in God's ways,
 God promises to feed us with finest wheat
 to satisfy our deepest needs.
My friends, in Christ, these promises are fulfilled.
In Christ, we are forgiven and made new.
Come, walk in the ways of the Lord!

Passing the Peace of Christ (Hebrews 13)
Let mutual love continue. Show one another signs of peace and love, for in doing so we may be entertaining angels.

Response to the Word (Hebrews 13, Luke 14)
My friends, we know what is good: to do justice,
to love mercy, and to walk humbly with our God.
 May mutual love and genuine hospitality
 be our guiding lights.
All who exalt themselves will be humbled,
but those who humble themselves will be exalted.
 May humble servanthood be our way
 in the world.

THANKSGIVING AND COMMUNION

Invitation to the Offering (Hebrews 13)
The letter to the Hebrews reminds us: "Keep your lives free from the love of money, and be content with what you

have." In contentment and gratitude, let us offer a portion of God's gifts to the ministry and mission of Christ's church.

Offering Prayer (Psalm 81, Hebrews 13)
Bless these gifts, O God,
as a sacrifice of praise and gratitude.
Through our generosity,
feed others with your finest wheat
and your sweetest honey.
Through our gifts,
may others find hope,
even in the rocky terrain of life
and the barren desert of despair.
May our lives be a sign of grace
to a world in need of your love. Amen.

SENDING FORTH

Benediction (Hebrews 13, Luke 14)
Go forth with the love of God,
sharing hope and hospitality
with all you meet.
Go forth with the grace of Christ,
giving kindness and compassion
to a world in need.

CONTEMPORARY OPTIONS

Contemporary Gathering Words (Psalm 81)
Hungry for God's nourishment?
Come with open mouths.
Hungry for God's love?
Come with open hearts.
Hungry for God's wisdom?
Come with open minds.
Come! Feast upon the finest of wheat,
the bread of Christ's mercy.

Come! Feast upon the sweetest of honey,
the hope of God's justice.
Come! Walk in the ways of our Lord.

Praise Sentences (Psalm 81)
Sing aloud to God!
Shout with praise and joy!
Sing aloud to God!
Shout with praise and joy!

SEPTEMBER 5, 2010

Fifteenth Sunday after Pentecost

Mary J. Scifres

COLOR

Green

SCRIPTURE READINGS

Jeremiah 18:1-11; Psalm 139:1-6, 13-18; Philemon 1-21; Luke 14:25-33

THEME IDEAS

The harsh path of following God emerges as a primary theme in today's scriptures. Jeremiah prophesies of a God who shapes evil against the Israelites because of their evil ways. The psalmist reminds us of how intimately God knows our every thought and deed. Paul writes to Philemon of a struggle about slavery. In Luke, Jesus calls us to hate the people and things we love in order to carry the cross of discipleship. These are not easy passages, nor is the path of following God. Yet, the path is truly the path of life; the path of fulfillment; the path of becoming the people we were created to be.

INVITATION AND GATHERING

Call to Worship (Psalm 139, Luke 14)
Searching, seeking, wondering, thinking,
we come to find our God.

Calling, crying, praying, singing,
we come to worship the Lord.
Walking, running, wandering, straying,
we yearn to follow Christ.
Bring your questions and open your hearts,
for God has invited us here.

Opening Prayer (Psalm 139, Luke 14)
Creative and creating God,
give us hearts and minds
that hear and respond
to your call in our lives.
Strengthen us in this time of worship,
that we may walk in your ways.
Shape us for discipleship,
that we may take up our cross
and follow Christ.

PROCLAMATION AND RESPONSE

Prayer of Confession (Psalm 139, Luke 14)
Gracious God,
search our hearts.
Root out the thoughts and plans
that draw us away from you.
Forgive us, O God,
for clinging to the things of our lives;
for holding onto our need for control;
for denying the cross you would have us bear;
for choosing paths that seem easier or safer
when you call us to the path of discipleship.
Guide us back to you,
and shape us in your image,
that we may be your people—
a people that bears the cross
with love and compassion.

Words of Assurance (Jeremiah 18)
As we turn from evil,
Christ reclaims us as children of God.

In Christ's mercy and forgiveness,
we are formed anew in the image of God.

Passing the Peace of Christ (Philemon)
Just as we remember one another in our prayers, take time
to remember one another with signs of grace and peace.

Response to the Word (Psalm 139, Luke 14)
God of knowledge and truth,
you search our hearts
and know our every thought.
You, who formed us in your image,
are shaping us even now.
Mold us ever more into your likeness.
Frame us into the wonderful creatures
you would have us become.
Weave us together to be your people,
that we may walk in your ways
and follow your path of truth.

THANKSGIVING AND COMMUNION

Offering Prayer (Jeremiah 18, Philemon)
Generous and loving God,
we thank you for the many joys
and signs of encouragement in our lives.
With these gifts,
create signs of encouragement and joy
in the lives of others
and in the ministries of our church.
In Christ's name, we pray. Amen.

SENDING FORTH

Benediction (Luke 14, Philemon)
Go forth as disciples of Christ.
Carry the cross of love and compassion
into our world of hatred and strife.

May the grace and peace of God
guide you on your way.

CONTEMPORARY OPTIONS

Contemporary Gathering Words (Jeremiah 18, Luke 14)
Come to Christ, who calls us by name.
We walk on the path of the cross.
Come to God, who shapes our lives.
We walk on the path of the cross.
Come to the Spirit, who molds our hearts.
We walk on the path of the cross.

Praise Sentences (Psalm 139)
How wonderful is our God!
How amazing are God's ways!
How wonderful is our God!
How amazing are God's ways!

SEPTEMBER 12, 2010

Sixteenth Sunday after Pentecost

Mary J. Scifres and B. J. Beu

COLOR

Green

SCRIPTURE READINGS

Jeremiah 4:11-12, 22-28; Psalm 14; 1 Timothy 1:12-17;
Luke 15:1-10

THEME IDEAS

What a fascinating contrast of images between our Hebrew and Christian scriptures today. Jeremiah prophesies
punishment and desolation, and the psalmist speaks of an
earth devoid of God's followers. But Paul writes of amazing grace, and Jesus promises rejoicing in heaven for forgiven sinners. As a sweep through salvation history, these
scriptures remind us that the journey of faith is one of fail-
ure and forgiveness—a journey involving both judgment
and mercy.

INVITATION AND GATHERING

Call to Worship (Psalm 14, 1 Timothy 1)
Rejoice, O daughters of Zion!
  Sing praise, O sons of Israel!
For in Christ, we are children of God.
  In Christ, hope is born again!

Rejoice, O daughters of Zion!
Sing praise, O sons of Israel!
For in Christ, we find refuge and strength.
In Christ, love is born again!

Opening Prayer (Psalm 14, Luke 15)
O God of heaven and earth,
look upon us now
with mercy and grace.
Enter our hearts
and make us holy.
Be our Shepherd
and guide us in your ways,
that we may no longer wander alone.
Hear our cries
and gather us to yourself,
that we may be one with each other
through the power of your Holy Spirit.
Amen.

PROCLAMATION AND RESPONSE

Prayer of Confession (Jeremiah 4, Psalm 14)
God of wind and fire,
blow through our lives;
release us from all that binds us;
free us from thoughts and fears
that keep us from union with you;
lay waste the burdens that impede us;
wash away the debris that weighs us down.
As we strive to follow your path,
guide us into the company of the righteous,
that we may be a refuge to the poor,
a deliverer to the captives,
and a friend to those who are alone.
In hope of your mercy, we pray. Amen.

Words of Assurance (1 Timothy 1)

Rejoice and be glad!
Christ Jesus, the promise of God's love, saves us—
even from ourselves!
Rejoice and be glad!

Response to the Word (Jeremiah 4)

We are lost, O God.
A scorching wind has blown through our lives,
leaving our souls a desert.
We look to your heavens above,
but the stars and moon
are shrouded from our sight.
Even the sun's rays are fruitless and dark.
In this world of sorrow and strife,
we yearn for your word of hope;
we yearn to hear your encouragement:
"Hold fast, the end is not yet come."
We cling to your word of hope, O God,
that we may find new life and new beginnings;
that we may be your people;
that you may be our God.

THANKSGIVING AND COMMUNION

Offering Prayer (Psalm 14)

O Lord, our God,
you have ever been our resting place.
When we had nothing to eat,
you fed us from your hand
and restored our fortunes.
When we were strangers,
you made us family.
Receive these gifts,
that all may know
we worship the living God.

SENDING FORTH

Benediction (1 Timothy 1, Luke 15)
Christ has welcomed us here.
The Spirit sends us forth.
God has called us to serve.
Christ has shown us how.
The Spirit has made us whole.
Love sends us forth!

CONTEMPORARY OPTIONS

Contemporary Gathering Words (Luke 15)
Are you lost and alone?
God is looking for you.
Come to the Shepherd of love!
Come to the Shepherd of love!
Are you afraid and far from home?
God is looking for you.
Come to the Shepherd of love!
Come to the Shepherd of love!

Praise Sentences (Psalm 47, 1 Timothy 1)
Rejoice in the Lord.
Rejoice and be glad!
Rejoice in the Lord.
Rejoice and be glad!
Rejoice in the Lord.
Rejoice and be glad,
now and forevermore!

SEPTEMBER 19, 2010

Seventeenth Sunday after Pentecost
Erik J. Alsgaard

COLOR
Green

SCRIPTURE READINGS
Jeremiah 8:18–9:1; Psalm 79:1-9; 1 Timothy 2:1-7;
Luke 16:1-13

THEME IDEAS
Stewardship runs through today's readings. How we
manage our time, talents, gifts, and service matters, for all
that we have and enjoy in this life are gifts from God.
Stewardship is, after all, a kingdom activity. Jeremiah implores us to hear the cry of the poor. The psalmist warns
us not to squander God's inheritance. In Luke, Jesus challenges us to be as wise as the dishonest manager. These
are issues worthy of serious study and reflection, issues
worthy of thoughtful worship.

INVITATION AND GATHERING

Call to Worship (Psalm 79, Jeremiah 8, Luke 16)
O God, we come into your courts
with praise and thanksgiving!
We come in celebration and song.

We come in gratitude of your inheritance.
We come as those who have received blessing
upon blessing.
We hear the cry of the poor in the land,
and ache to offer them relief.
We come to bring them blessing upon blessing,
in Jesus' name.
O God, we come into your courts
with praise and thanksgiving!
We come in celebration and song.

Opening Prayer (Jeremiah 8–9)
Gracious God,
    your people are suffering.
Where there is woundedness,
    help us bring healing.
Where there is discouragement,
    help us bring support and comfort.
Where there is dismay and mourning,
    help us bring the power of new life
        and new opportunities.
Heal us, O God,
    for you are our help and our hope,
    the One we turn to in times of trouble.
In the name of our Great Physician, Jesus Christ,
    we pray. Amen.

PROCLAMATION AND RESPONSE

Prayer of Confession (Jeremiah 8–9, Psalm 79, 1 Timothy 2, Luke 16)
We see the healing you offer us, O God,
    but find your cure hard to take;
    the quick fixes of this world
        seem so much more alluring.
Forgive us when we forget
    that you alone can heal us.

Forgive our hesitation
   to take the medicine you prescribe,
   for you are our one true physician,
      the source of all health and wholeness. Amen.
(B. J. Beu)

Assurance of Pardon

The One who weeps for us and for our world
   is the God of compassion,
      ever ready to meet us
      and to forgive our failings. Amen.
(B. J. Beu)

Passing the Peace (Psalm 79)

The Lord is the rock of our salvation, the One who delivers us from sin. In God's name I invite you to stand and greet one another. The peace of Christ be with you.
   In the name of the God of our salvation,
   peace be with you.

Response to the Word (Luke 16)

We seek to serve you, O God,
   by serving others:
   the poor, the needy, the least, and the lost.
Help us hear anew your words,
   that we may become more faithful stewards
      of the gifts you give us each day,
      through Jesus Christ our Lord. Amen.

THANKSGIVING AND COMMUNION

Invitation to the Offering (Luke 16)

God, in Jesus Christ, has given us much to be faithful for. Our tithes, gifts, and offerings may seem little in comparison to God's gifts to us, but we are called to be faithful over all that we have: our time, our talents, our gifts, and our service. When we give of ourselves, we practice the spiritual discipline of stewardship. When we are faithful

over a few things in this life, in the life to come we may be
faithful over much, much more. May God bless us in our
giving, that God's kingdom may be here with us on earth.

Offering Prayer (Luke 16)

Lord, we got up this morning,
  ate our breakfast, got dressed,
  and came to church—
    all to give you praise and thanksgiving.
May these gifts be a blessing
  for those who had no bed this morning
    from which to arise;
  for those who had no breakfast
    and are hungry this day;
  for those who have no new clothes;
  for those who long to worship you
    but cannot.
Take these gifts and use them
  as you will, O God.
In Jesus' name we pray. Amen.

Great Thanksgiving (Luke 16, Psalm 79)

The Lord be with you.
  And also with you.
Lift up your hearts.
  We lift them up to the Lord.
Let us give thanks to the Lord our God.
  It is right to give God our thanks and praise.
It is a right and good thing
  to give our thanks and praise to God,
  who made heaven and earth and all that is in it.
God commanded humankind
  to have dominion over the earth,
  to produce from its bounty
  a life of sharing and community,
  that all may find a saving relationship with God.
Through our sin, we have defiled the earth,
  and threaten our own existence with ruin.

Through our greed, ignorance, and hate,
  we have defiled God's gifts to us,
Yet, through it all, God's love never failed,
  even to the point of sending Jesus Christ
  to be our new life and salvation.
By delivering us from captivity to sin,
  God has remained faithful to us,
  tempering anger with grace and mercy.
And so, with your people on earth,
  and all the company of heaven,
  we praise your name
  and join their unending hymn, saying:
  Holy, holy, holy Lord, God of power and might,
    heaven and earth are full of your glory.
  Hosanna in the highest.
  Blessed is the one
    who comes in the name of the Lord.
  Hosanna in the highest.

SENDING FORTH

Benediction (Luke 16)
  By our words and deeds, we show God
  that we are faithful with the gifts we have received.
    Whether over a little or a lot,
    we seek to be faithful stewards of God's gifts.
  Take the gifts of God into the world,
  remembering the poor, the least, and the lost.
    We will take God's gifts to a hurting world,
    spreading a healing balm in all that we do.
    Praise be to God!

CONTEMPORARY OPTIONS

Contemporary Gathering Words (1 Timothy 2)
  Come to knowledge of the truth.
  Come to Jesus, the Christ.
    There is one God, and there is one Son,
    Jesus, the Christ!

Come to knowledge of the way.
Come to Jesus, the Christ.
There is one God, and there is one Son,
Jesus, the Christ!
Come to knowledge of the savior of the world.
Come to Jesus, the Christ.
There is one God, and there is one Son,
Jesus, the Christ!

Praise Sentences (1 Timothy 2)

There is one God, greatly to be praised!
There is one God, greatly to be praised!
There is one Son, greatly to be praised!
There is one Son, greatly to be praised!

SEPTEMBER 26, 2010

Eighteenth Sunday after Pentecost

Matthew J. Packer

COLOR

Green

SCRIPTURE READINGS

Jeremiah 32:1-3a, 6-15; Psalm 91:1-6, 14-16;
1 Timothy 6:6-19; Luke 16:19-31

THEME IDEAS

These passages present the benefit of a life connected to God
and the consequences of living disconnected from God.
Psalm 91 speaks poetically of the protection offered under
God's wings for those who trust in God. First Timothy in-
structs us that our top priorities should include righteousness, godliness, faith, love, endurance, and gentleness. One
of our "disconnects" centers around money. The rich man in
Luke is condemned because he did not use his money to
help his neighbor. Jeremiah metaphorically portrays God's
desire that humanity turn from its disconnectedness. The
prophet is instructed to purchase the land as a symbol of
God's "right of redemption" and as a promise of hope for
those who have chosen paths that have led them from God.

INVITATION AND GATHERING

Call to Worship (Psalm 91)
Those who dwell in the shelter of the Most High
will abide in the shadow of the Almighty.
They will say of the Lord, "God is my refuge
and fortress, the one in whom we trust."
Those who dwell in the shelter of the Most High
will abide in the refuge of God's wings.
They will not fear the terror of the night
nor the arrow that flies by day.
"Those who love me, I will deliver," says the Lord.
O Lord, we call to you now.
Show us your salvation.

Opening Prayer (Jeremiah 32, Psalm 91)
God our Redeemer,
    you promise deliverance to those who love you.
Draw unto us as we draw unto you in worship.
Open our eyes to see, our ears to hear,
    our minds to comprehend,
    and our spirits to encounter
        the revelation you have for us this day.
Transform us with the truth of your love and grace,
    in the name of the one who loved us
        and gave his life for us. Amen.

PROCLAMATION AND RESPONSE

Prayer of Confession (Luke 16, 1 Timothy 6)
Gracious and generous God,
    you lavishly bestow the gift of your love.
Forgive us, we pray—
    when we don't see or recognize your gifts
        for what they are;
    when we think we have somehow earned
        or are entitled to your generosity;
    when we take what you give
        and beg you for more;

when we hoard our gifts
and do not hear the mournful cry
of those around us;
when our desire for more
plunges us into ruin and destruction.
Teach us the ways of godliness,
and grant us a spirit of contentment,
that we may be grateful for your provision
and share the gifts you give with others.
As we are blessed by you,
so may we be a blessing to others,
in the name of your matchless gift,
our Savior Jesus Christ. Amen.

Words of Assurance (1 Timothy 6)

People of God, do not set your hopes
on the uncertainty of riches,
but rather on the richness of God,
who provides us everything for our enjoyment.
Be rich in good works, generous, and ready to share.
In the name of Jesus Christ, we are forgiven.

Passing the Peace of Christ (1 Timothy 6)

As we are commanded to share, let us turn to our fellow
pilgrims on the journey and offer one another the peace
of Christ.

Response to the Word (Luke 16)

God of Abraham, of Moses and the prophets,
we pray that your word will not fall on deaf ears,
on closed minds, on hardened hearts.
May the truth that is spoken today
transform our minds and our hearts,
unveiling the richness of your love,
the depth of your grace,
and the goodness of your mercy. Amen.

THANKSGIVING AND COMMUNION

Invitation to the Offering (1 Timothy 6)
Scripture reminds us that we brought nothing into the world and take nothing out of it. If we have food and clothing, we are to be content with these. We are told in scripture to do good, to be rich in good works, and to be generous and ready to share. For when we do good deeds, are rich in good works, and are generous and sharing, we store up the treasure of a good foundation for the future. We take hold of life that really is life. *Life that really is life.* What does that look like to you? Perhaps your offering today will help bring this life to someone else. What greater gift can we give?

Offering Prayer (Psalm 91)
God, our refuge and fortress,
    our deliverer and protector,
we thank you for hearing our call
    and for rescuing us.
We thank you for the gift of our salvation.
Bless now these gifts that we offer back to you—
    the gifts of our resources,
    the gifts of our hearts.
Use these gifts so that others may come to know
    the life that really is life. Amen.

SENDING FORTH

Benediction (1 Timothy 6)
People of God, pursue righteousness, godliness, faith,
    love, endurance, and gentleness.
Fight the good fight.
Take hold of eternal life.
To God, who dwells in unapproachable light,
    and to Jesus Christ, the blessed Sovereign,
    the King of kings and Lord of lords,
    and to the Spirit, be all honor and glory,
    now and forever.
Amen.

CONTEMPORARY OPTIONS

Contemporary Gathering Words (Psalm 91)

(Response may be spoken or sung.)
I will live in the shelter of the Most High
and abide in the shadow of the Almighty.
I will call upon the Lord.
The Lord is my refuge and fortress,
my God in whom I trust.
God is worthy to be praised.
The Lord will save me from the snare of the fowler,
from the terror of the night and the arrow that flies by day.
So shall I be saved from my enemies.
The Lord lives!
Let the God of my salvation be exalted.

Praise Sentences (Psalm 91)

God delivers and protects us.
Praise be to God!
God saves us in times of trouble.
Thanks be to God!
God satisfies us with the gift of our salvation.
Glory be to God!

OCTOBER 3, 2010

Nineteenth Sunday after Pentecost /
World Communion Sunday

Mpho A. Tutu

COLOR
Green or White

SCRIPTURE READINGS
Lamentations 1:1-6; Psalm 137; 2 Timothy 1:1-14;
Luke 17:5-10

THEME IDEAS
The readings from Lamentations and Psalm 137 speak of
the reversal of fortune. They speak of a people who have
lived in comfort and wealth but who must now endure
poverty and displacement in exile. In many places in the
world today, war and natural disaster have brought many
people accustomed to the good life face-to-face with the
reality that no human institution can guarantee either
safety or security. Nothing can guard our earthly treasures, and no person can promise world peace. But the
grace of God in Jesus Christ guarantees the eternal treasure that has been entrusted to us. Jesus is the author and
guarantor of true peace.

INVITATION AND GATHERING

Call to Worship (Lamentations 1, 2 Timothy 1)
The promises of the world turn to ashes and dust,
but the promises of God last forever.

The Holy One calls to us: "Come!"
**We come to rekindle the gift of God
ablaze within us.**

Opening Prayer (Lamentations 1, 2 Timothy 1)
Source of grace and peace,
    you call us into being;
    you keep us in safety;
    you hold us in life.
Far too often, we turn from you,
    placing our trust in the frail promises
        of other human beings
            and the insecure security of wealth.
Be with us now.
Bring us into your presence.
Comfort our pain.
Challenge our pride.
Enter into our prayer and our praise,
    that our worship may be pleasing to you.
We pray these things
    in the name of the one who loved us first,
        Jesus Christ.

PROCLAMATION AND RESPONSE

Prayer of Confession (Lamentations 1)
With the weepers we weep.
With the warriors we yearn for peace.
With the exiles we wander far from home,
    for our hearts wander far from you.
We live in an uncertain world—
    time and again we turn to people
        who promise us security.
But God, you are our only source of safety.
Help us turn to you,
    our heart's true home.
Call us again and lead us home.
Author of peace,
    teach us to seek our peace in you.

Source of every blessing,
 forgive us for the multitude of our transgressions.
Rekindle a spirit of love and self-discipline within us,
 through Jesus Christ, the Prince of Peace.

Words of Assurance (2 Timothy 1)
Our Savior Jesus Christ abolished sin and death
 and brought life and immortality to light.
By the grace of the Eternal One,
 we are forgiven in the power of the Holy Spirit
 living within us.

Passing the Peace of Christ (2 Timothy 1)
Hear the words of Jesus: "Peace I leave with you; my peace I give to you." The peace of Christ is ours, through the Holy Spirit who dwells within us.

Response to the Word (2 Timothy 1)
May we be people of living faith. May we live as people of gospel power. May we embody the spirit of self-discipline and love—the spirit that is ours by the grace and power of God, through Jesus Christ.

THANKSGIVING AND COMMUNION

Invitation to the Offering (Lamentation 1)
What will buy us peace? What is the price of security? What do we have, what can we hold onto, that will ensure that we will live all our days in comfort? What do we own that is not a gift from the One of abundant grace? Nothing we can own will buy true peace. Real security is priceless. Only the Holy Spirit, the Comforter, can assure us that we will be comfortable or comforted. All things come from the One of abundant grace. Let us give generously, in token of the abundance of our thanks.

Offering Prayer (2 Timothy 1)
Fount of blessing,
 you pour upon us
 the abundance of your grace.

Bless us and these gifts,
that they may be a source of blessing to others,
in the name Jesus Christ. Amen.

SENDING FORTH

Benediction (2 Timothy 1)
God has given us a spirit of power and love.
Let us go forth into the world
in the power of God's Spirit.

CONTEMPORARY OPTIONS

Contemporary Gathering Words (2 Timothy 1)
What do we need to be secure?
A good retirement plan, a strong dollar,
a solvent Social Security program?
What do we need to feel safe?
A strong police force, bold political leaders,
good intelligence on our enemies,
a well-guarded neighborhood?
These can all disappear in a moment.
Where then will we turn for help?
We will turn to our God,
the One who brings the captives home,
the One who brings life out of death.
Put your trust in the Lord.
(B. J. Beu)

Praise Sentences (2 Timothy 1)
Worship the Lord.
Worship the God of our ancestors.
Worship Christ, who rekindles our faith.
(B. J. Beu)

OCTOBER 10, 2010

Twentieth Sunday after Pentecost
Rebecca J. Kruger Gaudino

COLOR

Green

SCRIPTURE READINGS

Jeremiah 29:1, 4-7; Psalm 66:1-12; 2 Timothy 2:8-15;
Luke 17:11-19

THEME IDEAS

Our readings remind us that wherever we are hemmed in
and restricted, God is there in freedom. Jeremiah writes to
the Jews in Babylon that they are to make a home in the very
place to which they have been exiled—and they are to pray
for this city! The author of 2 Timothy writes of his chains as
a life-giving and freeing participation in the rejection and
death of Christ Jesus. To lepers who must keep their distance from everyone, Jesus speaks words of healing, oblit-
erating the distance between them. However we may be
bound, "the word of God is not chained" (2 Timothy 2:9),
and the locked iron door of impossibility swings open.

INVITATION AND GATHERING

Call to Worship (Psalm 66)
Make a joyful noise to God, all the earth!
Come and see what God has done!

God has turned our sea into dry land.
We have passed through the river on foot.
Bless our God, O peoples.
Let the sound of God's praise be heard!
When you tested and tried us, O God,
you brought us out to a spacious place.
You kept us among the living
and prevented our feet from slipping.
Make a joyful noise to God, all the earth!
How awesome are the deeds of our God!

Opening Prayer (Psalm 66, 2 Timothy 2)
We give praise to you, O God,
    for you are awesome and amazing.
We remember your deeds and faithfulness—
    deeds that have brought us to this day,
    faithfulness that has helped us weather
        life's storms.
We have gone through fire and water,
    and stand before you today
        in gratitude and praise.
How awesome are your deeds, O God! Amen.

PROCLAMATION AND RESPONSE

Prayer of Confession (Jeremiah 29, Psalm 66, 2 Timothy 2, Luke 17)
O God,
    we remember times of blessing in our lives:
        when we have been released
            from suffering and despair,
        when we have been freed
            to reclaim life and hope;
    but we also remember times of hardship:
        when we have been cast out
            into deep waters,
        when we have been banished in exile
            from the world we call home.

O God,
    it is hard to claim
        the hope and promise of the past
            in the presence of today's troubles.
Meet us today with your good news
    that we may be renewed
        by the power of your presence. Amen.

Words of Assurance (Psalm 66, 2 Timothy 2, Luke 17)
Give praise to God,
    who accompanies us on our journey,
    who hears our cries and anguish,
    and who remains faithful and answers our prayers.
Give glory to God,
    who brings life out of death
    and joy out of sorrow!

Response to the Word (Jeremiah 29, 2 Timothy 2, Luke 17)
Look to God in all the places you feel hemmed in and
bound, exiled and isolated. Open your eyes to God's presence. Trust God in the deepest parts of your being, that
silently or boldly, your life may reflect the Spirit of the One
who makes us whole. Amen.

THANKSGIVING AND COMMUNION

Invitation to the Offering (Luke 17)
When the leper ran back to thank Jesus for healing, new
life, and fresh possibilities, Jesus was amazed and moved
that a Samaritan would come to a Jew and give heartfelt
thanks. Jesus sent this man on his way with blessings, for
he saw that healing had permeated this man. He was
whole through and through. We too have known the healing and saving God in our lives, and we *will* know this
God yet again. So let our offering today be our thanksgiving for the mercy and goodness and ever-faithfulness
of God.

Offering Prayer (Jeremiah 29, 2 Timothy 2, Luke 17)
In a world of goodness and struggle,
we are grateful for your blessings, O God.
As we seek to endure life's struggles,
as we seek to claim your life
in those hard parts of our lives—
the very places you teach us
to look for your freeing presence—
teach us to trust that you are always there.
May these gifts be sent into our community
and into the world around us,
that others may claim
the hope of your presence. Amen.

SENDING FORTH

Benediction (Luke 17)
Jesus said to the leper,
"Get up and go on your way.
Your faith has made you well."
Let us all claim Jesus' healing
and liberation in our lives.
Get up and go on your way!
In Jesus' name,
your faith has made you whole
And all God's people say:
Amen.

CONTEMPORARY OPTIONS

Contemporary Gathering Words (2 Timothy 2, Luke 17)
Jesus, Master, have mercy on us!
**Where we need healing,
make us whole!**
Jesus, Master, have mercy on us!
**Where we are isolated and excluded,
bring us near!**

Jesus, Master, have mercy on us!
Where we are chained,
break our bonds!
Jesus, Master, have mercy on us!
Where we are dying,
bring us back to life!

Praise Sentences (2 Timothy 2)

If we have died with him,
we will also live with him.
If we endure,
we will also reign with him. Amen!

OCTOBER 17, 2010

Twenty-first Sunday after Pentecost
Bill Hoppe

COLOR
Green

SCRIPTURE READINGS
Jeremiah 31:27-34; Psalm 119:97-104; 2 Timothy 3:14–4:5;
Luke 18:1-8

THEME IDEAS
The word of God connects today's readings. Jeremiah
paints a beautiful image of the word being written on the
very hearts of God's people, a foreshadowing of the beginning of John's Gospel, where Jesus is described as the
Living Word come to dwell within us. The psalmist declares the importance of the word as the source of understanding, wisdom, and guidance. Paul writes to Timothy
about the word as the basis for sound teaching, reproof,
and correction. In Luke, Jesus tells the parable of the per-
sistent widow to teach us about patient, persevering
prayer. Throughout these readings God's word is revealed
as the foundation of our relationship with God.

INVITATION AND GATHERING

Call to Worship (Psalm 119, Jeremiah 31)
How beautiful is the word of the Lord!
How wise are God's commandments!

Through the Lord's precepts, we gain understanding.
Through God's wisdom, we find truth.
The Lord is our God; we are God's people.
God's word lives within us,
for it is written on our hearts.
Living Word, Great Teacher, lead us and guide us!
Amen!

Opening Prayer (Psalm 119, 2 Timothy 3–4)

Lord,
    your words are sweet to the taste,
        sweeter than honey;
    let them be our daily meditation and our study.
Give us ears to hear,
    for we marvel at your instruction.
Train us in righteousness,
    grant us patience and persistence,
        and equip us for every good work.
Inspire our faith,
    and give us voices to proclaim your message.
Guide our feet,
    keep us from every false way,
        for you alone speak the words of life. Amen.

PROCLAMATION AND RESPONSE

Prayer of Confession (2 Timothy 3–4, Luke 18)

From the least of us, to the greatest, Lord,
    we want to know you;
    we yearn to follow where you lead us;
    we need your guidance.
But even as we listen for your direction,
    other voices compete for our attention
        with teachings that suit our desires.
Our thoughts drift so far from your truth,
    that fables and fancies begin to seem real.
Holy One,
    open our hearts and minds.

By your Spirit,
   convince, rebuke, and encourage us
      as only you can;
   teach, correct, and inspire us
      in the ways of your salvation. Amen.

Words of Assurance (Jeremiah 31, Luke 18)
When we cry out, God helps us without delay.
Do not lose heart, for the Lord forgives our iniquity
   and remembers our sin no more.

Response to the Word (Jeremiah 31, 2 Timothy 3–4)
Lord, your word forms a strong foundation
   on which to build our lives.
Like a sower,
   you have planted your truth and your law of love
      in our very souls.
Watch over what you have planted
   and nurtured within us.
Find us faithful, O God,
      that we may take what we have learned
         and grow to know you.
For you are the One to whom we belong,
   the One to whom we pray. Amen.

THANKSGIVING AND COMMUNION

Offering Prayer (Psalm 119, Jeremiah 31)
Gracious God,
      you have granted us wisdom,
         understanding, and knowledge
            far greater than that of any teacher;
      you have given us love and grace
         freely from your abundance.
As you have shared your gifts with us,
   we share these gifts with you,
      that all the world may know you.
As you have led us by the hand,
   we offer our hands to your service,
      in praise and thanksgiving. Amen.

211

SENDING FORTH

Benediction (Psalm 119, Jeremiah 31, 2 Timothy 3–4)
May the living word of the Lord dwell with you.
May it live through you.
May it fill your thoughts and deeds.
May it fill your mouth with God's message of love.
May it sustain you in good times and bad.
May it equip you for a ministry of peace and hope!

CONTEMPORARY OPTIONS

Contemporary Gathering Words (Psalm 119)
Guided by the wisdom of the ages,
   we follow God's path.
Turning neither left or right,
   we keep God's ways.
Understanding the needs of our hearts and minds,
   we dwell in God's word.

Praise Sentences (Psalm 119)
How sweet are God's words,
sweeter than honey!
   How sweet are God's words,
   sweeter than honey!

OCTOBER 24, 2010

Twenty-second Sunday after Pentecost

B. J. Beu

COLOR

Green

SCRIPTURE READINGS

Joel 2:23-32; Psalm 65; 2 Timothy 4:6-8, 16-18; Luke 18:9-14

THEME IDEAS

God enters our struggles and brings rejoicing. In Joel, the Israelites, who had suffered long years of drought, are given life-giving rain. What's more, they receive the promise of new life in the form of prophecy, dreams, and visions. The psalmist rejoices in the bounty of God's blessings upon the earth. Even as Paul contemplates his martyrdom, he rejoices that he has finished the race in faith and will receive the crown of righteousness from our glorious God. In Luke, Jesus chastises those who build themselves up, but offers forgiveness to those who humble themselves before God. Even in the worst of times, God never abandons us. This is good news indeed.

INVITATION AND GATHERING

Call to Worship (Joel 2, Psalm 65)
Rejoice and be glad in the Lord.
God is our hope of our salvation.

The Lord blesses the earth with rain.
God crowns the year with bounty.
The Lord silences the roaring seas.
God quiets the tumult of the people.
The Lord gifts us with visions and dreams.
God takes away our shame.
Rejoice and be glad in the Lord.
God is our hope of our salvation.

Opening Prayer (Joel 2, Psalm 65, 2 Timothy 4)
Gracious God,
    we are tired from fighting the good fight;
    we are exhausted from running the race;
    we are weary from keeping the faith.
We need your care, O God.
We need your quiet center
    to silence the tumult of our lives.
We need your Spirit:
    to bless us with prophesy,
    to revive our dreams,
    to guide us with visions.
Nurture us with the rains of your love,
    that we may stay strong until the end,
        when we will be crowned
        with your righteousness. Amen.

PROCLAMATION AND RESPONSE

Prayer of Confession (Luke 18)
Merciful God,
    it is easier to think ourselves righteous
        than to admit our failings;
    it is easier to regard others with contempt
        than to see our own hypocrisy;
    it is easier to fret about having enough
        than to rejoice at your bounty.

Forgive our transgressions
and purify our hearts,
that we might be humble servants,
grateful for your love and care. Amen.

Assurance of Pardon (2 Timothy 4)
In Christ, there is reserved for us
a crown of righteousness,
which we share with all those who love him
and long for his appearance.
The one who answers our prayers for deliverance
has fitted us for the kingdom.
Rejoice and be glad!

Response to the Word (Ephesians 1)
Hold fast to the promises of God. God has poured out the
Spirit on all flesh. Our sons and our daughters shall
prophesy. Our men and women shall dream dreams. Our
people shall see visions. Hold fast to the promises of God.
Hold fast and live.

THANKSGIVING AND COMMUNION

Offering Prayer (Psalm 65, Luke 18)
Bountiful God,
we are overwhelmed by your generosity.
You water the earth with live-giving rain.
You clothe the meadows with flocks.
You deck the valleys with grain.
You crown the year with your bounty.
We give you thanks, O God,
and return to you the fruit of our labor
on this good, green earth.
Receive our gifts with humble thanks,
and receive our hearts into your keeping. Amen.

SENDING FORTH

Benediction (2 Timothy 4)
Fight the good fight. Finish the race. Keep the faith!
God is the hope of our salvation.
Place your trust in the One who crowns us
with righteousness.
To God be the glory, forever and ever.
Go forth to prophesy, to dream dreams,
and to see visions.
God is the hope of our salvation.

CONTEMPORARY OPTIONS

Contemporary Gathering Words (Joel 2, Psalm 65, 2 Timothy 4)
Our God is awesome and worthy of praise.
In the Spirit of Christ, we dream dreams.
In the Spirit of the Holy One, we see visions.
In the Spirit of Truth, we prophesy.
In Christ, we run the race.
In the Spirit of God, we keep the faith.
Our God is awesome and worthy of praise.

Praise Sentences (Psalm 65, 2 Timothy 4)
Be glad and rejoice in the Lord.
Give God the glory, forever and ever!
God is our hope and our salvation.
Give God the glory, forever and ever!
God crowns us with righteousness.
Give God the glory, forever and ever!

OCTOBER 31, 2010
All Saints Sunday
B. J. Beu

COLOR
White

SCRIPTURE READINGS
Daniel 7:1-3, 15-18; Psalm 149; Ephesians 1:11-23;
Luke 6:20-31

THEME IDEAS
In the face of persecution and evil, God is with those who
maintain their faith. Indeed, God's blessings extend to the
meek, the poor, the hungry, and those who have been per-
secuted for their faith. God does not leave us comfortless,
but offers us a glorious inheritance through Christ, who is
seated at the right hand of God in heaven. All Saints Day is
a perfect occasion to lift up those who have died in the faith.

INVITATION AND GATHERING

Call to Worship (Psalm 149)
Praise the Lord! Sing to the Lord a new song.
Rejoice and be glad, for the Lord reigns.
Praise God with dance.
Praise God with songs of adoration.
For God lifts up the lowly
and casts down the mighty.

The Lord adorns the humble with victory
  and visits judgment upon the proud.
Praise the Lord! Sing to the Lord a new song.
  Rejoice and be glad, for the Lord reigns.

Opening Prayer (Luke 6)

God of our forbearers,
  you turn our world upside down.
The world teaches us to trust our wealth,
  our social status, and our reputation,
  but you teach us that these things
    do not lead to life.
The world teaches us to focus on our needs,
  our wants, and our desires,
  but you teach us to focus on your kingdom,
    where the poor, the hungry, the sorrowful,
    and those persecuted for the gospel
      receive your blessing.
Help us live, as Christ taught us to live,
  that we may follow the example of the saints,
  who show us the way. Amen.

PROCLAMATION AND RESPONSE

Prayer of Confession (Luke 6)

Spirit of Truth,
  forgive our selective reading of your word.
We love to hear words of comfort:
  "Blessed are you who are poor,
    for yours is the kingdom of God."
But we shrink from words of judgment:
  "But woe to you who are rich,
    for you have received your consolation."
We are quick to ease the conscience of the rich,
  but slow to ease the plight of the poor.
Forgive our failings and strengthen our resolve,
  that our lives may bear witness
    to the fullness of your truth. Amen.

Assurance of Pardon (Ephesians 1)

Hear the good news.
In Christ, we have received an inheritance
   of God's redeeming love.
Through the gift of the Holy Spirit,
   we have been sealed in God's saving love. Amen!

Response to the Word (Ephesians 1:13-14)

We have heard the word of truth, the gospel of our salvation. May our hearts be marked by the seal of the Holy Spirit, which is the pledge of our inheritance as God's own people—a people redeemed and fitted for praise.

THANKSGIVING AND COMMUNION

Offering Prayer (Psalm 149, Luke 6)

God of abundant love,
   hear the song of our hearts:
      a song of thankfulness and praise,
      a song of hope and expectation,
      a song mixed with laughter and joy,
      a song filled with mirth and good will.
May the song of your love
   sing forth into the world
      through the gifts of our tithes and offerings.
May the joy of our hearts break forth—
   in acts of comfort to those who weep,
   in acts of mercy to the poor and imprisoned,
   in acts of encouragement to the weary.
We ask this in Jesus' name,
   the one who opened our hearts
      to see your love. Amen.

SENDING FORTH

Benediction (Psalm 149)

Go with God's blessing.
God's love surrounds us.

Go with God's blessing.
God's joy lifts us.
Go with God's blessing.
God's hope nurtures us.
Go with God.

CONTEMPORARY OPTIONS

Contemporary Gathering Words (Daniel 7)

My spirit is troubled; evil is afoot.
God alone can save us.
My spirit is troubled; nations rise against nation.
God alone can set things right.
My spirit is troubled; the innocent are devoured.
God alone can heal our wounds.
My spirit is troubled; will we receive the kingdom?
God alone can lead us home.

Praise Sentences (Psalm 149)

Praise the Lord!
Sing to the Lord a new song!
Dance and sing before the Lord.
Praise the Lord with drum and guitar.
Let the faithful rejoice in God's glory.
Praise the Lord!

NOVEMBER 7, 2010

Twenty-fourth Sunday after Pentecost
Mary J. Scifres

COLOR
Green

SCRIPTURE READINGS
Haggai 1:15b–2:9; Psalm 145:1-5, 17-21; 2 Thessalonians 2:1-5, 13-17; Luke 20:27-38

THEME IDEAS
Late in the season after Pentecost, lectionary scriptures focus on the coming of Christ. Seen as pre-Advent scriptures, today's readings foreshadow the promised birth of Jesus. Seen as Kingdomtide scriptures, these scriptures prepare us for the second coming of Christ, when God's realm shall finally come to fruition upon this earth. To prepare, whether for the celebration of Christmas or for the hope of God's promised reign, we are called to view the world with hope, trusting in God's presence and promise in our lives and in our world.

INVITATION AND GATHERING

Call to Worship (Psalm 145)
Praise to our God, our King, and our Lord.
Bless God's name forever!
For great is the Lord, glorious and just.
Bless God's name forever!

Opening Prayer (Haggai 1, Luke 20)

Ever-present God,
 be with us now
  in this time of worship;
  reveal your presence with us
  in this place of prayer.
In these days of preparation,
  reveal your justice and mercy.
Strengthen us to live as people of your promise,
  that we may be people of the age to come—
  people of justice and righteousness,
  people of faith and joy.
May it be so, O God;
  may it be so.

PROCLAMATION AND RESPONSE

Prayer of Confession (Haggai 1, Luke 20)

God of the ages,
 give us the courage
  to face these days unafraid;
 give us the strength
  to face our sins and our fears;
 give us the humility
  to admit our failures
   and acknowledge our weaknesses.
As we reflect upon our lives and confess our sins,
  hold us in your strong arms of love.
(Silent prayer of confession may follow.)

Words of Assurance (Psalm 145)

Know that the Lord is near.
God hears the cry
  of all who call upon God's holy name.
In confessing our sins,
  God saves and redeems us.
In the name of Jesus Christ, we are forgiven!

Passing the Peace of Christ (2 Thessalonians 2)
Forgiven and made whole in Christ Jesus, we are also made one family under God's guidance. Giving thanks for our sisters and brothers here, let us share signs of peace and joy with one another.

Response to the Word (Haggai 1, Psalm 145)
Take courage, my friends. God is with us. God's spirit abides in us. Even as God shakes the heavens and the earth, God's promises remain steadfast and true. Let us respond to God's word with courage and hope, trusting that God watches over us.

THANKSGIVING AND COMMUNION

Invitation to the Offering (1 Thessalonians 2)
Come, dear friends, you have been chosen by God as the first fruits of salvation. Through the blessing of the Spirit, and through our faith in God's truth, let us return a portion of the many gifts in our lives. Let us remember that we ourselves are gifts of God to be shared with the world.

Offering Prayer (Haggai 1)
Gracious God,
    you have filled this house
        with your splendor;
    you have filled our lives
        with abundance and grace.
Transform these gifts we return to you,
    that they may glorify you
        and shine your light upon the world.
Transform our very lives,
    that we too may be filled with your splendor
        and reflect your glory and grace. Amen.

The Great Thanksgiving (An Act of Preparation for Holy Communion)
The Lord be with you.
And also with you.

Lift up your hearts.
We lift them up to the Lord.
Let us give thanks to the Lord our God.
It is right to give our thanks and praise.
It is right and a good and joyful thing
    always and everywhere to give thanks to you,
    Almighty God, creator of heaven and earth.
In ancient days, you created us in your image
    and invited us to be reflections of your glory.
When we fell short and dimmed the brilliance
    of your light shining through us,
    you held our hands and walked with us
    out of the garden and into all the corners
    of the earth.
Through the ages, you have guided us
    in times of darkness and in times of discipleship.
Even when we turn away from you,
    you continue to walk with us
    and to extend the hand of your steadfast love.
In the words of the prophets,
    you offered your wisdom and your truth.
And in the fullness of time, you sent your Son
    Jesus Christ to reveal your grace in the world.
Even now, as we await your promised return,
    we remember your promises with trust and hope.
And so, with your people on earth,
    and all the company of heaven,
    we praise your name
    and join their unending hymn, saying:
    Holy, holy, holy Lord, God of power and might,
        heaven and earth are full of your glory.
    Hosanna in the highest.
    Blessed is the one
        who comes in the name of the Lord.
    Hosanna in the highest.
Holy are you and blessed is your salvation and grace,
    through Jesus Christ.

He who was and is the resurrection and the life
   has called us to be people of the resurrection,
   your church upon this earth.
Chosen as your first fruits for salvation
   through sanctification by the Spirit
   and through belief in the truth,
   we are your people, and we rejoice
   in your promise.
With joy and gratitude, we break this bread
   and remember the night when Jesus broke bread,
   gave it to the disciples, and said,
   "Take, eat; this is my body, which is given for you.
   Do this in remembrance of me."
With joy and gratitude, we take this cup
   and remember the night when Jesus took the cup,
   gave thanks, gave it to the disciples, and said,
   "Drink from this all of you;
   this is my blood of the new covenant,
   poured out for you and for many
   for the forgiveness of sins.
   Do this in remembrance of me."
And so, in remembrance of these
   your mighty acts of love and grace,
   we offer ourselves in praise and thanksgiving
   as your people, your children of hope and promise,
   as we proclaim the mystery of our faith.
   Christ has died. Christ is risen.
   Christ will come again.

SENDING FORTH

Benediction (1 Thessalonians 2)
   Now may the love, grace, and hope of Christ Jesus
      comfort your hearts and strengthen them
         in every good work and word.
   Go forth, as people of the promise,
      trusting in God's love as we share good works
         and Christ's saving love with the world.

CONTEMPORARY OPTIONS

Contemporary Gathering Words (Haggai 1)

Do you remember days of glory, long gone?
Do you yearn for a simpler time, a better life?
"Take courage," says our God,
    "a new day is dawning."
God's promises have yet to unfold.
The age to come holds the promise
    of justice and peace.
Take courage, and trust in the Lord!

Praise Sentences (Psalm 145)

Great is the Lord!
    Bless God's holy name!
Great is the Lord!
    Bless God's holy name!
Great is the Lord and greatly to be praised!

NOVEMBER 14, 2010

Twenty-fifth Sunday after Pentecost
Joanne Carlson Brown

COLOR
Green

SCRIPTURE READINGS
Isaiah 65:17-25; Isaiah 12; 2 Thessalonians 3:6-13;
Luke 21:5-19

THEME IDEAS
A new heaven and a new earth...wars and persecutions...they don't seem to go together. What were the lectionary folks thinking? These seemingly contradictory passages speak of endings and beginnings—the vision of what can and will be—times of trial, times of peace. It was the best of times; it was the worst of times. It is the contradiction we live in every day. We are caught between despair and hope; caught between people who tell us to be realistic and our vision of a better life. We are caught between those who believe the world is going to hell, and those who see a different life—a better life, a life that can come to be, will come to be, if we only believe the promises of God and live into them.

INVITATION AND GATHERING

Call to Worship (Isaiah 12)
Come people of God; come and celebrate
God's gift of salvation.

We come without fear.
We come trusting in God.
Come people of God; hear God's promises
and witness God's mighty deeds.
In hearing the promises,
in witnessing the mighty deeds of God,
we are strengthened for all that lies ahead.
Come, let us worship and praise God
by shouting aloud and singing for joy,
for God truly is in our midst.

Opening Prayer (Isaiah 65, Luke 21)
Our loving and caring God,
we need this time together
to be united with our sisters and brothers
in the faith;
we need this time of worship
to be comforted and strengthened
in your presence.
We hear of wars and rumors of wars.
We read of persecution and oppression.
Remind us again of your vision,
that all might live in a world
of peace and justice and love.
May this time together
imprint this vision and promise on our hearts,
that we may live into this beloved community. Amen.

PROCLAMATION AND RESPONSE

Prayer of Confession (Isaiah 65, Luke 21)
O God, we are more like the vision in Luke
than the vision of Isaiah.
We see wars, hatred, and violence everywhere,
yet despair of ever stopping them.
We see oppression and injustice and persecution,
but fail to raise our voices in prophetic protest.
We have become a pessimistic people.

Help us believe—really believe—
in Isaiah's vision of the peaceable kin-dom,
in your promise of a new heaven and new earth.
Let your cry be our cry:
"They shall not hurt or destroy
on all my holy mountain." Amen.

Words of Assurance (Isaiah 12)
God is our strength and our salvation.
God's anger is turned away,
and in its place we find comfort,
steadfast love, and forgiveness.
With this hope, we can draw water
from the wells of salvation
with joy and thanksgiving.

Passing the Peace of Christ (Isaiah 65)
Sisters and brothers, we are part of the new heaven and
new earth. In God's love we can reach across the differ-
ences that divide us. Greet one another in this spirit of reconciliation and peace.

Response to the Word (Isaiah 65, Luke 21)
For these words of challenge and of hope,
we give you thanks and praise.
May they enable us to lead lives
that embody both challenge and hope,
bound together by your love.

THANKSGIVING AND COMMUNION

Invitation to Offering (Isaiah 65, Luke 21)
The world is a mess. What can we do? We can offer our visions of hope, our words of comfort, our acts of love, our
resources to help bring God's new heaven and new earth.

Offering Prayer (Isaiah 65)
O God,
we long to make a difference
in our world.

We offer you what we have:
   our visions and dreams;
   our witness to your saving acts
     of love and justice;
   our resources to help bring
     the new heaven and new earth
       into our midst.
We offer you our very lives,
   that we may be coworkers with you
     to bring about true change.

SENDING FORTH

Benediction (Isaiah 65, Luke 21)

Go forth into a world that needs new visions.
Bring the message of hope and love,
   of justice and peace, to all you meet.
Live the dream. Make it reality.
Celebrate endings and new beginnings,
   challenges and promises.
Live the new creation. Amen.

CONTEMPORARY OPTIONS

Contemporary Gathering Words (Isaiah 65)

Have you heard?
Something new is coming,
   a different world than the one we know.
And we're the ones to help make it happen!
Let us gather together,
   to support and encourage one another
   and to praise God—
     for new visions, for hope,
     for new beginnings, and for new possibilities.

Praise Sentences (Isaiah 12)

Sing praises to God who has done gloriously!
Shout aloud and sing for joy, for God is in our midst!
God is our strength and salvation.
I will trust in this and not be afraid.

NOVEMBER 21, 2010

Reign of Christ Sunday / Christ the King Sunday

Hans Holznagel

COLOR

White

SCRIPTURE READINGS

Jeremiah 23:1-6; Luke 1:68-79; Colossians 1:11-20;
Luke 23:33-43

THEME IDEAS

This is no ain't-broke-don't-fix-it Sunday, or even an
onward-and-upward perfecting of the present order Sunday. Ordinary time gives way to Advent, but for one week
we offer a prophetic salute to Christ's reign: no plea, no
mere hope or prediction, but rather a celebration that God
certainly will sweep away the old. The days are *surely*
coming, and they *will* be proclaimed: a new dominion of
just, righteous days; a rescue from oppressive powers;
light erasing death's shadow, even in the bitter plight of
one unjustly executed and sarcastically taunted as "king."

INVITATION AND GATHERING

Call to Worship (Jeremiah 23, Luke 1)
It is done.
God has always been in charge—
    yesterday and today.
Even when things seem out of control,
    God's reign is on its way.
Let us prepare the way for God.

Opening Prayer (Jeremiah 23, Colossians 1)
Faithful God, expand our thankful imaginations:
    to time beyond our time,
    to wisdom beyond our wisdom,
    to strength beyond our strength.
As we pray for your coming reign,
    remind us that the whole earth
        is already yours.
Even as we pray for things not yet seen,
    help us celebrate your sure, eternal reign. Amen.

PROCLAMATION AND RESPONSE

Prayer of Confession (Jeremiah 23, Colossians 1)
Imagining your reign
    can be difficult, eternal God.
It is difficult to picture a world
    governed by your justice
    and righteousness alone.
Our minds are held captive
    by the worst images
    of human kings, rulers, and powers.
When nobler visions fail
    and we settle for kingdoms
        of our own making,
        correct and forgive us.
Free the borders of our imaginations,
        that we may envision your greater good
            and celebrate the coming of your reign
                on earth as in heaven. Amen.

Assurance of Pardon (Luke 1)
Hear the prophecy of Zechariah:
Tender mercy and forgiveness
are the ways of God. We are forgiven.
Let the church say
Amen.

Response to the Word (Jeremiah 23)
May the word take root in our hearts, that we may be
fruitful bearers of God's wisdom. Amen.

THANKSGIVING AND COMMUNION

Offering Prayer (Jeremiah 23, Luke 23)
Your days are surely coming, Holy One,
just as surely as the needs of this world are real.
We offer these gifts
in awe of your victory over the cross
and in celebration
of your present and coming reign,
that life—even life abundant—
might multiply for all people.
Bless these gifts,
that they may be used
according to your will. Amen.

SENDING FORTH

Benediction (Colossians 1, Luke 1)
Go joyfully. Give thanks to God.
Endure with strength and patience.
And may your feet be guided in the ways of peace. Amen.

CONTEMPORARY OPTIONS

Contemporary Gathering Words (Jeremiah 23, Luke 1)
Amid the holiday rush, let's pause to reflect:
not yet on a stable, or star, or Advent candles,
or everything for which we're thankful.

Those days are surely coming, but others are as well:
days of holiness and righteousness,
salvation and safety, deliverance and rescue;
the dawn of a day when God's tender mercy
will trump oppression and death.
Such are the days of Christ's reign.
They are surely coming! Let's celebrate today!

Praise Sentences (Colossians 1, Luke 1)

God has raised up a mighty savior!
Prepare the way! Serve God without fear!
Thrones, dominions, rulers, powers—
these are all as dust before our God.
Prepare the way! Serve God without fear!
Praise be to God and the day of God's favor.
Prepare the way! Serve God without fear!

NOVEMBER 25, 2010

Thanksgiving Day
Leigh Anne Taylor

COLOR
White

SCRIPTURE READINGS
Deuteronomy 26:1-11; Psalm 100; Philippians 4:4-9;
John 6:25-35

THEME IDEAS
The theme of today's passages is God's provision and the
thankful response of God's people. Deuteronomy describes the liturgical act of offering first fruits to God, and
Psalm 100 may well have been the song of thankfulness
God's people sang as they offered their gifts. The Gospel
of John takes God's provision one step further: Jesus proclaims that he is the bread of life—the bread of God that
comes down from heaven, the bread that gives life to the
world. Philippians serves as a thankful, thoughtful response to God's gift of spiritual food in Jesus Christ.

INVITATION AND GATHERING
Call to Worship (Psalm 100, Philippians 4)
Rejoice in the Lord always.
    Again I say, rejoice!
God is good!
    God's love endures forever!

Give thanks to God.
God's faithfulness never ends!
Bless God's holy name.
Worship God with glad songs of joy!

Opening Prayer (Deuteronomy 26)
Eternal God,
apart from your gracious provision,
we have nothing;
how can we not worship you
this Thanksgiving Day?
We bow before your greatness
and proclaim you as our God.
Accept our offering of thanksgiving and praise,
and help all of our days be a living sacrifice
of our devotion to you. Amen.

PROCLAMATION AND RESPONSE

Prayer of Confession (Philippians 4)
Christ Jesus,
many of our thoughts are unworthy of you:
they are not true or honorable,
they are not righteous or pure,
they are not pleasing or commendable.
Forgive us for filling our minds with worry
and cluttering our focus with distractions
from daily life.
Help us focus on things
that are praiseworthy and lead to life.
Guard our minds,
that we may dwell on thoughts
that bring us closer to you. Amen.

Words of Assurance (Philippians 4:6-7)
"Do not worry about anything,
but in everything by prayer and supplication
with thanksgiving let your requests
be made known to God.

And the peace of God,
  which surpasses all understanding,
  will guard your hearts and your minds
  in Christ Jesus."
Beloved in Christ, receive forgiveness from God
  with thanksgiving and praise.

Passing the Peace of Christ (Philippians 4:9)
As the Apostle Paul reminds the church at Philippi: "Keep
on doing the things that you have learned and received
and heard and seen in me, and the God of peace will be
with you." The God of peace is with us! Let us greet one
another with words of God's peace.

Response to the Word (Deuteronomy 26, John 6)
Celebrate the bounty that God has given us
  in God's holy word.
  Thanks be to God.
Celebrate the true bread of heaven, the bread of life!
  Praise be to Christ.

THANKSGIVING AND COMMUNION

Invitation to the Offering (Deuteronomy 26)
In a moment, we will offer God ordinary offering plates
filled with our gifts of money. May these plates be for us
baskets, filled with the first fruits of the harvest. May these
plates reflect our gratitude for all that God has given us in
the promised land of our abundant lives. Let us offer our
first fruits with gladness.

Offering Prayer (Deuteronomy 26)
Holy God,
  with gratitude and thanks,
  we offer you the first fruits of your harvest.
We bow humbly before you,
  remembering all that you have done for us

and acknowledging that everything we have
comes from you.
With thanksgiving and praise,
we offer these gifts
to sustain and bless the work of your church
and to care for the poor. Amen.

SENDING FORTH

Benediction (Deuteronomy 26)
God's love and care never ends.
**May our lives be a thankful response
to God's nurture and bounty.**
Go in God's love and care, to love and care
for your neighbor.

CONTEMPORARY OPTIONS

*Contemporary Gathering Words (Deuteronomy 26,
Psalm 100, Philippians 4)*
Rejoice in the Lord all the time!
Rejoice, rejoice, rejoice!
Sing to the Lord your God.
Sing, sing, sing!
Worship the Lord with thankful hearts!
Worship with thanksgiving!

Praise Sentences (Psalm 100)
The Lord is God! The Lord is good!
God's love never changes!
The Lord is God! The Lord is good!
God's faithfulness lasts forever!
The Lord is God! The Lord is good!
God made us. We belong to God!

NOVEMBER 28, 2010

First Sunday of Advent
Mary J. Scifres

COLOR
Purple

SCRIPTURE READINGS
Isaiah 2:1-5; Psalm 122; Romans 13:11-14; Matthew 24:36-44

THEME IDEAS
Christmas is coming! The emphases of today's readings are different than we may be hearing and seeing in advertisements and at shopping malls. For Christians, the day of the Lord is coming. Christmas is a vivid reminder that not only has Christ come as a little child, but Christ comes again to fulfill the promise of God's realm on this earth. Advent is our season to prepare for this realm—where war will cease and people will walk in God's ways. As we prepare, we are called to be ready—to enter God's house, to worship, to pray, to walk in Christ's light, and to live as children of light. In doing so we usher in God's new world, the realm of hope and promise that Christ offers to this earth and its peoples.

INVITATION AND GATHERING
Call to Worship (Isaiah 2, Romans 13)
We know what time it is—
the moment to wake from sleep.

We awaken to greet the day,
yearning for God's peace on this earth.
Let us lay down our swords
and put aside all works of darkness.
Let us walk in the light
and live as peacekeepers.
Let us worship our God
as expectant believers.
We worship with joy,
knowing Christ will come!

Opening Prayer (Romans 13, Matthew 24)
Holy One,
we wait and hope for your peace.
We live in the promise of your love.
As the days darken and the nights lengthen,
light our way with your promised presence.
Prepare us to celebrate your birth,
and guide us to create your kingdom on earth.
In hopeful expectation we pray. Amen.

PROCLAMATION AND RESPONSE

Prayer of Confession (Isaiah 2, Romans 13)
Christ Jesus, we pray for light and guidance
in the darkness of our lives.
When we seek darkness,
bring us to the light.
When we walk paths of war and injustice,
guide us to your paths of love and mercy.
When we sleep through life,
awaken in us the desire to be your children.
Forgive us for taking pleasure in destruction
and for walking paths that distract others
from your ways.
Help us lay aside the works of darkness
and put on the protection of your light and love.
With hope, we pray for your gracious forgiveness
and your wise counsel. Amen.

Words of Assurance (Romans 13)
Let us lay aside the works of darkness!
Let us put on the armor of light!
For in Christ Jesus,
    we are forgiven and made new.
Salvation is nearer to us now
    than when we first believed.
And now, Christ invites us
    to be clothed in righteousness,
    to walk in the light of God!

Passing the Peace of Christ (Romans 13)
As children of light, let us lay aside all works of darkness
and greet one another with signs of light and love!

Preparing to Hear the Word of God (Psalm 122)
Were you glad when they said to you, "Let us go to the
house of the Lord!"? Take heart, my friends, for God's
house comes to us in the reading of scripture and the hearing of God's holy word. Be glad and rejoice! These words
are God's gift to us!

Response to the Word (Isaiah 2, Romans 13)
God of light and love,
    we have come to your mountain this day;
    we have heard your invitation
        to walk in your light.
Guide us now to be children of light,
    to awaken from the apathy
        that separates us from you
        and from one another.
As you teach us your ways,
    help us learn and grow
        as people of peace and hope. Amen.

THANKSGIVING AND COMMUNION

Offering Prayer (Romans 13, Matthew 24)
Although we do not know
    the day or time of your coming, dear God,

we know that now is the time
to be your children of light.
Receive the gifts we bring.
Transform them into light for the world,
into signs of peace and hope for all to see. Amen.

SENDING FORTH

Benediction (Romans 13)
Put on the armor of Christ's light.
Shine for all the world to see.
Go forth in the love of God!

CONTEMPORARY OPTIONS

Contemporary Gathering Words (Isaiah 2, Romans 13, Matthew 24)
About the day or hour, no one knows.
About Christ's love, we know even now!
About swords into plowshares, we can only hope.
About Christ's love, we know even now!
About nations at peace and salvation for all,
we may doubt.
About Christ's love, we know even now!
Come, let us go up to the mountain of God.
Let us look at the world through Christ's eyes.
Let us walk in the light of the Lord!

Praise Sentences (Psalm 122, Romans 13)
Rejoice, for God is near!
Rejoice, for God is near!
Be glad, take heart, and sing!
Be glad, take heart, and sing!

DECEMBER 5, 2010

Second Sunday of Advent

Joanne Carlson Brown

COLOR

Purple

SCRIPTURE READINGS

Isaiah 11:1-10; Psalm 72:1-7, 18-19; Romans 15:4-13;
Matthew 3:1-12

THEME IDEAS

Prophecy, promises, and preparation—all are part of the
Advent tradition. They serve as reminders in this hectic
season that there is more to prophecy than guessing what
is in this package; more to promises than what Santa
Claus will bring; more to preparation than cleaning house
and putting on a spread for a holiday party. On this second Sunday of Advent, we are called back to the longing,
not for a certain present, but for a messiah who brings
about a beloved community of harmony and peace—but
not without opposition. These passages speak of wishes,
desires, and the hint of fulfillment that is Christmas. We
need to hear, believe, and get ready.

INVITATION AND GATHERING

Call to Worship (Isaiah 11, Psalm 72, Matthew 3)
In this season of prophecy, promise, and preparation,
we come to be renewed and refreshed.

We come to be inspired by stories of a messiah
who will change the world—and change us.
We come to listen for words of hope and joy,
promise and challenge.
We come with open ears, open minds,
and open hearts. We come to receive
the blessings God has in store for us
in this season of waiting.
Come! Let us worship our God—
the One who brings all things to fulfillment.

Opening Prayer (Isaiah 11, Romans 15, Matthew 3)
God of hope and encouragement,
we come in the midst of this season
of busyness and preparations:
to find a time and space to slow down,
to reflect on what our true preparations
should be.
We need to prepare our hearts
to receive the gifts of love and hope.
We need to prepare our minds
to focus on your promise
that a messiah will come
and nothing will be the same.
We need to prepare our spirits:
to praise God for prophecy,
promises, and preparation;
to find hope and encouragement;
to find peace and joy.
May we do so now, in our time of worship. Amen.

PROCLAMATION AND RESPONSE

Prayer of Confession (Isaiah 11, Psalm 72, Matthew 3)
O God,
the stories of our faith have lost their power.
We have heard the prophecies spoken so many times,
the promises retold again and again,

the call to prepare ourselves for your coming
repeated so often,
we don't really hear or heed them anymore.
We have replaced these messages of life:
with guessing what presents we are getting,
with preparing for parties
and the social obligations of Christmas.
Bring us back to a sense of mystery:
a sense of awe, a sense of wonder,
a sense of excitement, a sense of anticipation,
a sense that something special
is about to break into our everyday world.
Help us prepare our hearts, souls, and minds
for the coming of the messiah. Amen.

Words of Assurance (Psalm 72)

God's promises are sure—
promises of steadfast love and forgiveness.
God deals with God's people
with righteousness and justice.
Rejoice and be glad!

Passing the Peace of Christ (Romans 15)

Paul urges the Romans to welcome one another, just as
Christ has welcomed them. Let us greet one another with
words and signs of peace and welcome.

Response to the Word

May these words of prophecy, promise, and preparation
encourage us to steadfast love and action.

THANKSGIVING AND COMMUNION

Invitation to Offering (Psalm 72)

Our God has done wondrous things, and has done them
for us. Let us respond to God's acts of love and wonder by
offering our whole selves, that God's promises might be
fulfilled through us.

Offering Prayer (Isaiah 11)
We thank you, Holy One,
for all your good gifts,
especially the gifts of prophecy, promise,
and calls for preparation.
As a thankful response to these gifts,
we offer our belief, our commitments, and our money,
that we may hasten the time
when no one will hurt or destroy
on all God's holy mountain.

SENDING FORTH

Benediction (Romans 15)
May the God of hope
fill you with all joy and peace in believing,
that you may abound in hope
by the power of the Holy Spirit. Amen.

CONTEMPORARY OPTIONS

Contemporary Gathering Words (Isaiah 11)
Get this! Someone special is coming—
someone who will be wise;
who won't judge on appearances;
who will live a good life;
who will bring about a time
when wolves and lambs,
leopards and goats,
cows and lions
all lie down together.
And we're invited to be there
to help make it happen.
So come and hear the stories again,
and get ready for quite a happening.

Praise Sentences (Psalm 72)
Blessed be God's glorious name forever.
May God's glory fill all the earth.
Amen and amen!

DECEMBER 12, 2010

Third Sunday of Advent

Laura Jaquith Bartlett

COLOR

Purple

SCRIPTURE READINGS

Isaiah 35:1-10; Luke 1:47-55; James 5:7-10; Matthew 11:2-11

THEME IDEAS

These Advent readings proclaim a world turned upside down. For those who are currently poor, hungry, or oppressed, this is great news. But for those who enjoy the comforts of food in abundance, warm places to live, steady jobs, and a voice in the political system, well, this means acknowledging our role in the world's injustices. Somehow the good news doesn't seem quite so good. But the scriptures call us to work side by side with Jesus in bringing about God's vision of abundance for all. When we claim our calling as partners in the dance, we can truly rejoice in the coming of Christ!

INVITATION AND GATHERING

Call to Worship (Isaiah 35)
In the midst of the barren land,
flowers burst into bloom.

In the midst of the dry desert,
streams of water gush forth.
In the midst of sorrow and sighing,
joy and gladness dance together.
We shall see the glory of God!

Opening Prayer (Isaiah 35)
God of Glory,
we rejoice in the good news
of your promises.
Come into our parched world
and shower us with your gushing,
abundant water of life.
Enter into our brokenness,
and renew us with the strength of your love.
Be born anew in our hearts
and in our world.
Come, Jesus; come.
We are ready! Amen.

PROCLAMATION AND RESPONSE

Prayer of Confession (Isaiah 35, Luke 1, Matthew 11)
Upside-down God,
you announce your coming with exciting news:
the hungry will eat their fill,
the oppressed will dance
in newfound freedom;
you proclaim your mission with hard news:
the well fed will go hungry,
the powerful will lose their status.
We find ourselves squirming
as we acknowledge our participation
in structures that oppress and marginalize.
Help us accept and proclaim
the coming of your Son
as truly good news.

Give us the courage
   to set aside our privilege,
   and help bring about this upside-down world,
      where everyone can sing together for joy.

Words of Assurance (Isaiah 35)

The desert shall rejoice and blossom.
Waters shall break forth in the wilderness.
The burning sand shall become a pool.
The God who can transform the dry lands
   can also transform the desert of our lives.
Abundant forgiveness is ours
      from the God who turns sorrow and sighing
         into joy and gladness.

Passing the Peace of Christ (Isaiah 35)

The coming of Christ turns the world upside down. For folks who are quite content with things as they are, this may not feel like good news! But a greater vision lies before us—God's vision of real life for all. Comfort one another with these words of encouragement: **"Be strong, do not fear."** Respond in kind with these words of hope: **"God will come and save you."**

Response to the Word (Luke 1, Matthew 11)

My soul magnifies the Lord.
   My spirit rejoices in God my Savior.
We will work with Christ to feed the hungry,
   for gluttons have no place at God's table.
We will work with Christ to lift up the lowly,
   **for the politics of power has no place
   in the realm of God.**
We will work with Christ to bring good news
to the poor,
   **for the love of Jesus Christ is too exciting
   to keep to ourselves.**
My soul magnifies the Lord.
   My spirit rejoices in God my Savior.

THANKSGIVING AND COMMUNION

Offering Prayer (Isaiah 35, Luke 1)
Generous God,
  you have given us all that we have
    and all that we are.
We thank you for the opportunity
  to respond to your love and generosity
    by sharing our gifts with others.
Our hearts sing with joy
  as we work with you
    to bring true peace and justice to our world.
As we prepare for the coming of your Son,
  may our lives proclaim your good news for all
    throughout the earth. Amen.

SENDING FORTH

Benediction (Matthew 11)
May the love of God fill you
  until you overflow with joy.
May the coming of the Christ Child free you
  to live in an upside-down world.
May the Holy Spirit empower you
  to work for the reign of God on earth.
At Christmas and throughout the year,
  may you be inspired to share the good news
    of God's vision of peace and love. Amen.

CONTEMPORARY OPTIONS

Contemporary Gathering Words (Matthew 11)
We hear the echo of a promise:
"I'm coming!"
  Are you really the One?
"The blind receive their sight and the lame walk."
  Are you really the One?

"The lepers are cleansed and the deaf hear."
Are you really the One?
"The dead are raised and the poor eat their fill."
But are you really the One?
"I'm the One who changes the world.
Are you really ready for me?"
**With God's help, we're ready to follow you.
We're ready for you!**

Praise Sentences (Luke 1)

My soul magnifies the Lord.
My spirit rejoices in God my savior.
For the Mighty One has done great things for me.
Holy is God's name.
My soul magnifies the Lord,
My spirit rejoices in God my savior.

DECEMBER 19, 2010

Fourth Sunday of Advent

B. J. Beu

COLOR

Purple

SCRIPTURE READINGS

Isaiah 7:10-16; Psalm 80:1-7, 17-19; Romans 1:1-7;
Matthew 1:18-25

THEME IDEAS

Isaiah promises the birth of Emmanuel—"God is with us."
The psalmist longs for God's light, for restoration, for salvation—for God to be with the people. Joseph dreams of
the child who will be called Emmanuel. And Paul witnesses to the blessings of this holy child. On this Sunday
before Christmas we speak of God with us—of a child
who brings light to our darkness, restoration to our ruin,
and salvation to our lives.

INVITATION AND GATHERING

Call to Worship (Isaiah 7, Psalm 80, Matthew 1)
Stir up your might, O God. Come and save us.
    In the bleak midwinter,
    let your face shine upon us.
Give us a sign that you are with us.
    Give us dreams of the birth of Emmanuel.

Send a little child to lead us—
  a child who knows how to refuse the evil;
a child who knows how to choose the good;
  a child of promise.
Stir up your might, O God. Come and save us.
  In the bleak midwinter
  let your face shine upon us.

Opening Prayer (Isaiah 7, Psalm 80)

Restore us, O Shepherd of Israel,
  like you restored your people of old.
Feed us no longer on the bread of tears,
  but on the power of your presence.
Teach us how to refuse evil
  and to choose the good.
Strengthen us in prayer.
Bless us with the joy of a little child—
  a child of promise,
  a child of hope,
  a child called Emmanuel, God is with us. Amen.

PROCLAMATION AND RESPONSE

Prayer of Confession (Isaiah 7, Psalm 80, Matthew 1)

O God,
  we are so easily distracted.
We go out of our way
  to see the beautiful Christmas lights,
  but we fail to see the light of the world,
    the light that came long ago
      through the birth of a child.
We hurry to finish our Christmas shopping,
  frantically seeking that perfect gift,
  but we have forgotten how to be still
    and treasure the Gift we have been given.
Forgive our angry tempers.
Overlook our impatience.
Teach us to see the signs of our salvation
  in the smiles of children everywhere. Amen.

Assurance of Pardon (Isaiah 7, Romans 1, Matthew 1)
Hear the message spoken through the prophets of old
  through the dreams and visions of the faithful.
God grants us grace and peace through Christ,
  that we may know that God is with us.

Response to the Word (Matthew 1)
The One who visited Joseph in a dream visits us still. The
Spirit that was at work saving the Hebrew people long
ago is at work in our lives today. The child born of Mary
is in our midst. Feel God's presence among us. Be restored
through the power of God's salvation.

THANKSGIVING AND COMMUNION

Offering Prayer (Psalm 80, Matthew 1)
Gentle Shepherd, we are the flock of your pasture.
No longer do we feed on the bread of tears,
  but on the promise of your presence.
Your Spirit guards and guides us.
In thankfulness and praise
  for the gift of a child born to us,
    receive our tithes and offerings.
Receive our hearts also,
  that we may live as those touched
    by your great gift. Amen.

SENDING FORTH

Benediction (Isaiah 7, Matthew 1)
In the bleak midwinter, God has given us a sign.
  A child shall be born for us.
He shall be called Emmanuel—God is with us.
  We go with anticipation and longing.
Go with joy and hope.
  We go trusting the promises of God.

CONTEMPORARY OPTIONS

Contemporary Gathering Words (Isaiah 7, Psalm 80, Matthew 1)
We await the birth of a child.
We can hardly wait.
We await the arrival of God's greatest gift.
We are ready to receive.
We await the one who is God with us.
We open our hearts to the Christ child.
We await the salvation of the world.

Praise Sentences (Isaiah 7, Psalm 80, Matthew 1)
God is with us!
Glory to God in the highest!
Christ is with us!
Glory to God in the highest!
Salvation is at hand.
Glory to God in the highest!

DECEMBER 24, 2010

Christmas Eve

Mary J. Scifres

COLOR

White

SCRIPTURE READINGS

Isaiah 9:2-7; Psalm 96; Titus 2:11-14; Luke 2:1-20

THEME IDEAS

Glory to God! Christ is born! Salvation is come to the earth! This message is more than just a familiar story. It is a message that invites us to sing loudest praises, proclaiming God's glory as angels and shepherds did so long ago. In the singing of carols and the proclaiming of God's good news, we are invited to remember why Christ came: to redeem us and purify us that we might be the people of God—people "who are zealous for good deeds" (Titus 2:14b). Even in the joyous celebration of Christmas, we are called to fulfill the message of justice and righteousness that Jesus lived in word and deed.

INVITATION AND GATHERING

Call to Worship *(Isaiah 9, Psalm 96, Luke 2)*

Sing to the Lord a new song!
Sing of Christ's glorious birth!
Sing praises with all of the earth!
Sing praises with the angels of heaven!
Declare God's glory on this night of nights!
Let God's glory shine all around!
Treasure these words and ponder the good news:
a child is born to us who is Christ the Lord!

Opening Prayer *(Isaiah 9, Titus 2)*

Wonderful Counselor,
  guide us this night
    and in this season of Christmas.
Mighty God,
  strengthen our hearts
    to live as redeemed people.
Everlasting Father,
  gather us in your arms,
  and help us remember
    that we too are your children,
    born anew through your gracious love.
Prince of Peace,
  abide in us
    with the peace that passes all understanding.
Shine in us this night,
  that we who walked in darkness
    may go forth as children of light!

PROCLAMATION AND RESPONSE

Prayer of Confession *(Isaiah 9)*

God of grace and glory,
  illumine our lives this night.
Too often, we have lost sight of your guiding star—
  we have been far too harried this month;

we have forgotten the message of peace, hope,
joy, and love, born this beautiful night;
we have neglected our relationship with you,
which draws us to this place;
we have neglected our relationships with others,
which nurture and strengthen us.
Forgive us, we pray—
when we walk in darkness;
when we no longer reflect your light
and your glory.
Bathed in your glorious light,
inspire us to live lives of love and joy.
Stir our hearts to return to you,
through the wondrous gift of Christ
born in us anew each day. Amen.

Words of Assurance (Titus 2, Luke 2)

As we receive God's grace and mercy,
we are reminded of angels and shepherds
and the words of comfort and joy:
"Do not be afraid; for see—I am bringing you
good news of great joy for all the people:
to you is born this day
in the city of David a Savior,
who is the Messiah, the Lord."
In Christ, we have received grace upon grace.
In Christ, salvation is available to all.
Praise to God, for in Christ we are forgiven!

Passing the Peace of Christ (Isaiah 9, Titus 2)

Children of light, share this joyous news with one another!
Love has come! Grace is ours! Christ is born this night!

Response to the Word (Isaiah 9, Titus 2)

Wonderful Counselor,
you have given us these precious scriptures
as gifts of grace and love.
Help us live the words you have given.
Help us walk in the light
you shine so brightly upon our world.

Purify us, Mighty God,
 that we may truly be your people—
  a people zealous for good deeds,
  a people striving for your realm of justice
   and righteousness upon this earth.

THANKSGIVING AND COMMUNION

Offering Prayer (Luke 2)
On this Christmas night,
 we offer ourselves and our gratitude
  in remembrance for your gracious presence
  in our lives and in our world.
Be born in us anew,
 and shine your light
  through these gifts we now bring.
Surround us with your glory,
 that we, like the shepherds long ago,
  might sing your praises and reveal your grace
   in all that we say and in all that we do.

The Great Thanksgiving (An Act of Preparation for Holy Communion)
The Lord be with you.
And also with you.
Lift up your hearts.
We lift them up to the Lord.
Let us give thanks to the Lord our God.
It is right to give our thanks and praise.
It is right, and a good and joyful thing,
 always and everywhere to give thanks to you,
 Mighty God, Wonderful Counselor,
 Everlasting Father, Prince of Peace.
In ancient days, you created us in your image
 to be reflections of your glory.
When we fell short and dimmed the brilliance
 of your light shining through us, you held our hands
 and walked with us out of the garden
 into all the corners of the earth.

When we were afraid to look upon your glory,
   you came as a quiet traveler, as a burning bush,
   and as a pillar of light.
You called us to be people of light,
   to walk no longer in darkness,
   and always, you light our way.
Even when we walk in darkness, you shine your light
   and offer your grace, awaiting our return to you.
In the fullness of time, you sent your Son Jesus Christ
   to reveal your glory and grace.
And so, with your people on earth
   and all the angels of heaven, we praise your name
   and join their unending hymn, saying:
   Holy, holy, holy Lord, God of power and might,
      heaven and earth are full of your glory.
   Hosanna in the highest.
   Blessed is the one
      who comes in the name of the Lord.
   Hosanna in the highest.
Holy are you and blessed is your salvation and grace,
   come to earth on this night long ago.
Born as a child, birthed in a stable,
   surrounded by the poorest of the poor,
   Jesus came with your message of loving grace
   to the humblest of all.
Through this child, we have seen your glory.
Through this child, we are invited into your presence,
   reconciled to your righteousness,
   and called forth to walk in your light.
With joy and gratitude, we break this bread
   and remember another night
   when your grace was revealed.
For on that night many years after Jesus' birth,
   Jesus took the bread, gave thanks to you,
   broke the bread, and gave it to the disciples, saying,
   "Take, eat; this is my body, which is given for you.
   Do this in remembrance of me."

With awe and wonder, we fill this cup and remember
    another night when your forgiveness was revealed.
For on that night many years after Jesus' birth,
    Jesus took the cup, gave thanks to you,
    and gave it to the disciples, saying,
    "Drink from this, all of you; this is my blood
    of the new covenant, poured out for you
    and for many for the forgiveness of sins."
And so, in remembrance of these your mighty acts
    of love and grace, we offer ourselves in praise
    and thanksgiving as your children of light,
    in union with the brightness of Christ's glory,
    as we proclaim Christ's birth and the mystery
    of our faith.
    Christ has died. Christ is risen.
    Christ will come again.

Communion Prayer (Isaiah 9, Titus 2)

Pour out your Holy Spirit on all of us gathered here,
    that we who walked in darkness
        might walk forth in the light of Christ.
Shine your Holy Spirit
    upon these gifts of bread and wine,
    that your glorious grace and love
        might flow through us
        as the very presence of Christ.
As we receive these gifts,
    may we shine forth as your people,
        that the glory of Christ might be revealed
        for all to see.

Giving the Bread and Cup

(The bread and wine are given to the people, with these or other words of blessing.)
The life of Christ, living in you.
The grace of God, flowing through you.

SENDING FORTH

Benediction (Titus 2, Luke 2)
Treasure these words:
   Christ is born.
   Light has shined,
      and the darkness cannot overcome it.
Ponder these thoughts:
   Christ is born.
   Love has come.
   Salvation is given to all!

CONTEMPORARY OPTIONS

Contemporary Gathering Words (Isaiah 9, Luke 2)
On this night of nights, a baby was born—
   a child wrapped in cloths has changed the world.
On this night of nights, light has shined—
   light radiating in the glory of a baby's birth.
God's children wrapped in love
   can still change the world!

Praise Sentences (Psalm 96, Luke 2)
Sing with the earth!
Sing praises to God!
Christ is born this day!
   Sing with the earth!
   Sing praises to God!
   Christ is born this day!

DECEMBER 26, 2010

First Sunday after Christmas Day
B. J. Beu

COLOR
White

SCRIPTURE READINGS
Isaiah 63:7-9; Psalm 148; Hebrews 2:10-18; Matthew 2:13-23

THEME IDEAS
The saving love of God unifies these readings. Isaiah proclaims that it was no angel that saved the people of old,
but the very presence of God. The psalmist praises God
over and over again: all creation, heaven and earth, young
and old, birds of the air and every creeping thing; they all
praise the Lord. How can we not join them? Hebrews depicts the suffering of Christ for our salvation, and
Matthew recounts Herod trying to rid the world of its redeemer by slaughtering the innocent. Salvation should be
treasured and celebrated, but it should never be taken
lightly—for it is costly.

INVITATION AND GATHERING

Call to Worship (Psalm 148)
Praise the Lord!
Praise the Lord from the highest heaven!
Let the sun and the moon and the stars in the sky
sing praises to our God!

Praise the Lord!
Praise the Lord from the deepest valley!
**Let the mountains and the hills, the fruit trees
and tall cedars, sing praises to our God!**
Praise the Lord!
Praise the Lord all the peoples of the earth!
**Let the old and the young,
the mighty and the meek, lift their voices
and praise God's holy name!**
Praise the Lord!

Opening Prayer (Isaiah 63, Hebrews 2, Matthew 2)
Gracious Savior,
it was no heavenly messenger or angel
that came into our lives to save us;
it was no passing fancy
that led to our freedom from captivity;
it was no painless gesture
that pioneered our salvation;
it was your very presence;
it was a plan with roots as deep as the sea;
it was an act of long-suffering love.
Be with us now,
as we praise you with our lips
and love you with all our heart.
Be with us now,
for we are your people,
and you are our God. Amen.

PROCLAMATION AND RESPONSE

Prayer of Confession (Matthew 2)
Holy One of God,
we rejoice with the angels
who proclaimed your birth
and saved your life,
but we pay little heed to the messengers
who proclaim your birth
to save our lives;

we celebrate the heavenly light
 that guided the wise to Bethlehem,
but we fail to see the light
 that can see us safely through
  our darkest journeys.
Open our eyes anew,
 that we might see the old stories come alive
 and find the grace we need
  to meet each day with hope and joy.

Assurance of Pardon (Isaiah 63, Psalm 148)
God is faithful and abounding in steadfast love.
In Christ, God has come to us to be our salvation.
In the birth of Jesus, God lifts us up
 and carries us all the days of our lives.

Response to the Word (Hebrews 2)
Jesus claims us as brothers and sisters, lifting us up before
God. Let us, in kind, lift up Jesus in the midst of this con-
gregation and offer him our praise.

THANKSGIVING AND COMMUNION

Offering Prayer (Isaiah 63, Psalm 65)
Glorious God,
 all life has its source in you.
Through you, the stars come into being
 and the waters cover the deep.
At your command, trees bear fruit
 and the earth provides food for your creatures.
Your steadfast love gives us everything we need.
In thankfulness and praise for your many gifts,
 we offer you our love, our service,
  and our offerings.
In the name of the one who came
 to be our salvation, we praise you. Amen.

SENDING FORTH

Benediction (Isaiah 63, Matthew 2)
As we go forth, more than a star guides us;
more than a messenger shows us the way;
more than an angel protects us from harm.
We go forth in the presence of the living God.
Go with the blessings of the one who is our life
and our salvation.

CONTEMPORARY OPTIONS

Contemporary Gathering Words (Psalm 148)
Praise God from the heavens above.
Praise God!
Praise God from the depths below.
Praise God!
Praise God from the love in your heart.
Praise God!
Praise God from the joy in your soul.
Praise God!
Praise God!
Praise God!

Praise Sentences (Christmas)
Christ is born.
Shout alleluia!
Christ is born.
Sing God's praises!
Christ is born.
Laugh with joy!

CONTRIBUTORS

Erik J. Alsgaard
Lakeland, FL

Laura Jaquith Bartlett
Lebanon, OR

Brian J. Beu
Laguna Beach, CA

Mary Petrina Boyd
Seattle, WA

John A. Brewer
Sammamish, WA

Joanne Carlson Brown
Seattle, WA

Shelley Cunningham
St. Paul, MN

Rebecca J. Kruger Gaudino
Portland, OR

Jamie Greening
Port Orchard, WA

Hans Holznagel
Cleveland, OH

Bill Hoppe
Duvall, WA

Sara Dunning Lambert
Duvall, WA

Marcia McFee
Truckee, CA

Shari Jackson Monson
Gig Harbor, WA

Matthew J. Packer
Swartz Creek, MI

Ciona Rouse
Nashville, TN

Bryan Schneider-Thomas
Kent City, MI

Mary J. Scifres
Laguna Beach, CA

Leigh Anne Taylor
Blacksburg, VA

Mpho A. Tutu
Alexandria, VA

SCRIPTURE INDEX

SONG AND HYMN INDEX

COMMUNION LITURGY INDEX

Includes prayers and liturgies in both the print text and the CD-ROM.

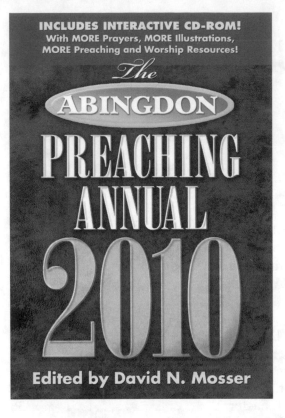

Preachers have long turned to *The Abingdon Preaching Annual* for help with the central task of their ministry: sermon preparation. The 2010 edition of the *Annual* continues this fine tradition with lectionary-based and topical sermons for flexibility in choice, additional lectionary commentary, and worship aids for every sermon. The CD-ROM, included with every book, provides classical and contemporary affirmations and prayers, plus hyperlinked planning aids such as bibliographical references, and the full lectionary texts for each Sunday. *The Abingdon Preaching Annual* is now one of the most comprehensive and useful resources for sermon preparation that you will find on the market.

"Commendations to Abingdon Press for offering two fresh ecumenical resources for pastors."

For *The Abingdon Preaching Annual*—"Anyone who dares proclaim a holy word week in and week out soon realizes that creative inspiration for toe-shaking sermons quickly wanes. Multitasking pastors who are wise seek out resources that multiply their own inductive initiatives."

For *The Abingdon Worship Annual*—"Not only the sermon but also the whole service dares to be toe-shaking . . . and the *Worship Annual* is a reservoir of resources in that direction."

—The Reverend Willard E. Roth, Academy of Parish Clergy President, *Sharing the Practice: The Journal of the Academy of Parish Clergy*

 Abingdon Press   w w w . c o k e s b u r y . c o m